The Fat Girl's Guide To Loving Your Body

K.L. Montgomery

Copyright © 2020 by K.L. Montgomery
All rights reserved. This book or any portion thereof may not be reproduced or used in any manner whatsoever without the express written permission of the publisher except for the use of brief quotations in a book review.

Printed in the United States of America

First Printing, 2020

ISBN 978-1-949394-07-8

Mountains Wanted Publishing
P.O. Box 1014
Georgetown, DE 19947
www.mountainswanted.com

Cover Designed by the Author

To anyone who has struggled to find your self-worth:
please know you are worthy of love

no matter your size

no matter your shape

no matter your weight.

Inspirational AF Playlist	viii
Start Here	1
Who are you and why should we listen to you?	4
How to Use This Book	7
Journaling Assignment #1: Thinking back...	9
The Misogynistic Myth of Feminine Beauty Standards	11
Time to Get Deprogrammed	14
Journaling Assignment #2: Messages	18
Why We Need to Reclaim the Word Fat	20
Can I Use This Book If I'm Not Fat?	22
What's the difference between Body Positivity and Fat Acceptance?	23
Your Relationship With Food	25
Journaling Assignment #3: Tell Me About Your Mother, I Mean, Your Relationship with Food	28
What is Diet Culture and Why Is It So Harmful?	30
Meet Your New Body	33
Journal Assignment #4: Photo-Journaling	36
Let's Start at the Bottom and Work Our Way Up	38
Journaling Assignment #5: Feet & Legs	40
I Like Big Butts and I Cannot Lie	42
Journaling Assignment #6: Doin' the Butt	44
Waist, Abdomen, and Hips	46
Journaling Assignment #7: Waist, Belly & Hips	48
Arms, Shoulders & Back	50
Journaling Assignment #8: Arms, Shoulders & Back	51

THE FAT GIRL'S GUIDE TO LOVING YOUR BODY

Boobs: You Knew This Was Coming 53

Journaling Assignment #9: Your Breasts 55

Face, Hair, and Neck, OH MY! 57

Journaling Assignment #10: Face, Neck and Hair 60

Hey, you know something I forgot? Body Hair 62

Saving the Best for Last: Your Insides 64

Journaling Assignment #11: It's What's on the Inside That Counts 66

Now Let's Put it All Together 67

Dealing with Body- and Fat-Shamers 101 68

Hey, Were You Aware You're Fat? 69

But You're Glorifying Obesity! 70

But You Have Such a Pretty Face 71

I Wish I Had Your Confidence 72

But I'm Concerned About Your Health! 73

Journaling Assignment #12: A Letter to Body- and Fat-Shamers 75

Dealing with the Medical Community 76

So what if you do want to lose weight? 79

Journaling Assignment #13: All the Diets 82

More on Exercise 84

Female Stuff 87

Journaling Assignment #14: Lady Parts 90

SEX! (Yes, I'm Going There)— Oh, and Relationships 92

Journaling Assignment #15: Let's Talk About Sex, Baby! 96

Aging 98

v

Journaling Assignment #16: Aging Gracefully	101
Be A Good Role Model	103
Journaling Assignment #17: Role Models	105
Your Diet is Not Just Food	107
When Things Get Really Rough	111
Journaling Assignment #18: Identifying Triggers & Action Plan	117
Self-Care	119
Journaling Assignment #19: Make a Plan for Self-Care	122
Dressing Your Body	124
Journaling Assignment #20: Fashion Going Forward	127
It Costs Nothing to Be Kind, But It Does Take Some Work	129
Journaling Assignment #21: My Pledge to Be Kind	132
Building Your Tribe	133
Journaling Assignment #22: Building Your Tribe	136
Your Official Invitation to Join My Fat Girl's Tribe!	138
But wait, there's more!	139
Daily Bopo Meditations	142
YOU DID IT!	326
Acknowledgments	327
About the Author	328
Also By K.L. Montgomery	329

THE FAT GIRL'S GUIDE TO LOVING YOUR BODY

Inspirational AF Playlist

Fuckin' Perfect – P!nk

Scuse Me – Lizzo

Body Love Part 1 – Mary Lambert

Big Girl (You Are Beautiful) – Mika

Try – Colbie Caillat

***Flawless – Beyoncé

Scars to Your Beautiful – Aleesia Cara

Born This Way – Lady Gaga

Love Myself – Hailee Steinfeld

Woman Up – Meghan Trainor

Beautiful – Christina Aguilera

Brave – Sara Bareilles

This Body – Baum

Thunder Thighs – Miss Eaves

Shameless – Lissie

Video – India Arie

Fat Bottomed Girls – Queen

Start Here

So…

You bought this book. Or maybe someone bought it for you (if so, wow, kinda presumptuous, huh?)

And now you're cracking it open and thinking, *well, maybe I'll give it a shot.*

Maybe it's time to finally learn how to love my body. After all, I've been living in it for X years, and hating it hasn't worked out too well.

Maybe this K.L. Montgomery lady—if that is even her real name—can help me learn to love my body?

An aside: *Krista Lynne Montgomery* is the name on my birth certificate, so, yep, it's real, even if I'm married now and use a different name for things other than books. But it's kinda weird to be called K.L., so you can call me Krista if you'd like.

Anyway, you're skeptical about the claim this book makes, right? I don't blame you. I would be too.

Why is it so important to love your body? Why does it have to be *love*? I had someone ask me if *accepting* your body is good enough. What if you're just *neutral* about your body, will that work? Why does it have to be *love*?

I'm glad you asked. There are a couple of reasons, actually.

For one, we need to remember the difference between "like" and "love." If you're a mother, this will be an easy analogy for you to understand. You *love* your children unconditionally all the time. But that doesn't mean you always *like* them. It doesn't mean you don't want to spank them to kingdom come sometimes, or that you never want a break from them. But you always *love* them. Know what I mean?

Loving your body is the same way. You're not going to love it every minute, hour, or day. There are still going to be parts of it that bother you, things about it that drive you up the wall. But at the end of the day, you're never getting another body, so ultimately you gotta love the one you've got.

Secondly, we take care of things we *love* better than we take care of things we don't love (or feel neutral about). Why aim for feeling neutral or settle for mere acceptance when you could experience full-on unconditional love? That's what you'd say about a romantic relationship, right?

What if you were filled with so much love and respect for your body that you treated it with kindness, gentleness and filled it with whole foods that you enjoy eating and plenty of exercise that you also enjoy, and stimulated your brain with all sorts of awesome things (because, after all, your brain is a part of your body too, even if we do tend to think of it separately), and you consequently ended up living a long and happy life? Or, what if it wasn't even that long, but at least it was happy? No one sets out to live a miserable, pathetic, meaningless life, do they? We *all* want happiness. We *all* want meaning. And we deserve those things.

You can have more happiness and meaning in your life if you choose to love your body. Even though it's hard. Even though it's work. Even though you won't always *like* your body. The simple fact remains that loving your body leads to making the best choices for it, which will lead to a better life in the long run.

In the past, you might have had a set of conditions that needed to come to fruition before you could love your body. Do any of the following sound familiar?

If I just lose X pounds, I will be happy with my body.

If I just fit into my size X jeans again, I will love my body.

If I just work out hard enough and long enough, and can finally see my X (abs, collarbones, biceps, thigh gap, etc.), I will finally *love my body.*

*If I can just find someone *else* who loves my body, I will love it too.*

If you've been putting off living and enjoying your life because of any of those things, then I hate to break it to you, but YOU'RE MISSING OUT. Your life is happening right now. However old you are now? You're never going to be that age again. I don't wanna be all doom and gloom, but your life could be snatched away from you tomorrow. What if you did die tomorrow, and you never really enjoyed yourself because you thought you were too fat? It's a *heartbreaking* thought.

The time is now, my dear reader. The time to love yourself and to live your life to the fullest, no matter your size, your shape or your weight, is right this very minute. I hope if nothing else, this book reminds you of that fact. But, buckle up, buttercup, because there's a long, winding road ahead of you.

What if I told you that loving your body, *truly, unconditionally* loving your body…

…is a choice you need to make every single day?

…isn't something you can decide to do once and then you're good for the rest of your life?

…must truly be unconditional? If it's really going to stick, it has to be an unconditional love. You can't beat yourself up for having low days or binge days or days you can barely stand yourself. You just realize those days are a part of life, and you start fresh the very next day.

What if I told you that loving your body isn't an automatic thing? You don't just flip a switch and then BOOM, it's Self-Love City all up in here. It's something you'll have to work really hard at, and it will take time. This book is designed to be used over the course of an *entire year*, and even after completing every single journal assignment (and there are a BUNCH), you will still need to work at it.

What if I told you that once you learn to love your body that you might not *like* it some days? As a matter of fact, there might be times when you are still completely disgusted by it.

What if I told you there is no magic pill, no diet plan, no workout regimen, no doctor, no significant other, no fancy clothes that can *make* you love your body? In fact, it is entirely up to YOU and YOU ALONE.

Do you still want to give it a shot? Would you still like to get to the point where you aren't disgusted, ashamed, embarrassed, or mortified by the shell that houses your soul? Do you think it would be worth it, even with all the hard work, the two steps forward and one step back?

Well, you've come to the right place.

And trust me, it *is* worth it.

You're worth it. And I want to help you believe that.

Who are you and why should we listen to you?

It's a valid question. You just put a few bucks in my pocket by buying this book, and you must have thought you'd get something out of it, but you also may have wondered why I think I'm an authority on the subject. I'm going to start by telling you what I'm *not* an authority on, and what I *can't* help you with. Yeah, I do things ass-backwards sometimes.

First off, I'm not a psychologist. I do have a bachelor's degree in psychology that I earned from Indiana University in 1996. But you know how bachelor's degrees are. They really just mean I took like twelve psych classes that I remember slightly better than the two years of French and Calculus I took. I couldn't tell you shit about Calculus—I'm gonna be up front about that right here and now! I also have a master's degree in library science—in a former life, I was a research librarian. Not that you give a single fuck about that.

(Oh, BTW, I curse sometimes. #sorrynotsorry. If you're super offended by curse words, this is probably not the book for you.)

Secondly, I'm not a doctor. I have had zero medical training, so I'm not going to give you medical advice. If you have medical issues, you should *definitely* see a doctor. However, I do have firsthand knowledge of the way the medical community treats people of size, and you better believe I'm going to call out their lying, prejudiced, body-shaming asses in this book. *rubs hands together with glee*

Thirdly, I'm not a lawyer, so I'm not going to give you any legal advice, nor should anything I say be construed as legal advice. Why would I even bring that up? Well, because by the time we're done here, you may be feeling a wee bit litigious and wanting to sue the pants off people who have been outright lying and bullshitting you for your entire life—yes, that list includes doctors, parents, teachers, friends, and other *supposedly* well-meaning assholes. Not to mention the entire diet industry. Now, those fuckers actually *should* be sued. But I digress. I'm not a lawyer. Let's leave it at that for now.

Whew, okay, enough of that. I sound a little angry, huh? I am. I am angry, and here's why:

A lot of my life was stolen from me by people who made me feel like I wasn't good enough because I'm fat.

When I was ten or eleven, my mother put me on my first diet. When I was twelve, thirteen, fourteen, I was bullied about my weight by my peers. If you've ever read my book *Fat Girl*, the scene where Claire is harassed by the boys at the fast food restaurant? That actually happened to me when I was in junior high.

When I was almost fifteen, I decided I was tired of being fat, so I limited my diet to lettuce, grapes, rice and frozen yogurt, if I even ate at all. I exercised for at least two hours a day: running, swimming, weightlifting, aerobics. I weighed myself and took my measurements at least three times a day and charted all of that plus my calories in journals. I lost forty pounds in two months, going from 174 pounds to about 135. Guess what? I STILL FELT FAT.

All through high school and college, I constantly yo-yoed between 135 and 175. Back and forth, back and forth. Then, at age twenty-two, I got pregnant with my first son. I gained a staggering eighty pounds. But after he was born, I went back to my starvation and over-exercise routine and lost all the weight within nine months. In 1999, I suffered from several miscarriages, piling on a lot of the weight I'd lost before getting pregnant with my second son, who was born in 2000. I ended up weighing 275 after he was born. It took me longer to lose the weight, but thanks to my foolproof routine of starving myself and exercising multiple hours a day, I lost well over a hundred pounds before he was eighteen months old.

The sick, sick thing is that starving myself gave me a high. Seeing that needle move down lower and lower was a rush I couldn't replicate with anything else. I was obsessed.

Then I had son number three and ended up right back at 275.

I never did lose all the weight after he was born. I think I got down to 205 at my smallest, but my body was like "what the fuck is wrong with you?" It just refused to cooperate with my tried and true methods of starvation and over-exercise. Sure I'd lose twenty pounds here or there, but as soon as I even attempted to eat normally again, boom, I'd gain more than I'd lost in the first place.

Yo-yo dieting and starving myself had destroyed my metabolism.

It wasn't until 2015 that I decided enough was enough. By that time, my third son was ten, so I'd spent ten long years battling my "baby weight," and I almost weighed as much as I had when he was born.

How much did I miss out on during those ten years? How many events did I not attend or did I just lurk in the background because I was ashamed of my weight? How many times did I shy away from being who I really am because I was afraid people would judge me? How many times did I feel worthless, undesirable, and unlovable because of the number on the scale or the size of my jeans?

Too. Many. Damn. Times.

That's when I wrote *Fat Girl*. That's when I realized that happiness is MY choice. Loving my body is MY choice. Letting others dictate the way I feel about myself is MY choice. Not wearing certain clothing or not putting myself in certain situations because of my weight is MY choice.

I was tired of the mentality that if I just lost X pounds, I would be happy. That I would go on that trip. That I would buy myself that dress. That I would do any number of things when I finally reached my goal weight.

I had been waiting TEN YEARS for that to happen, and it hadn't! I was forty-one years old at that point. I'd lost what might have been the best decade of my life because I refused to cut myself some slack and realize the number on the scale or the tag in my jeans said nothing about what kind of human I was or what I deserved out of life.

If you are in that wasteland, that pit of loneliness, unworthiness, and depression that I was drowning in those ten years, I want you to know that it is possible to pull yourself out. All of those feelings you have about your stomach, your thighs, your loose or sagging skin, your stretch marks, your cellulite, I have had them too. And I'm here to tell you that it does not matter one iota what you weigh or what your body looks like, there is a beautiful soul inside that body who is deserving of every happiness.

And it's time for her to put on her crown and reign.

How to Use This Book

Okay, so we're in agreement that you need to make a change to your mindset. I cannot possibly stress two things to you enough:

1. That it's indeed your mind that needs to change, not your body.
2. *I* cannot change your mindset for you. Only *you* can do it. That's why this book is interactive, meaning it has a journaling component.

I could cite a bunch of scientific research that corroborates my statement that journaling can help improve your self-actualization and help you stick to your goals. Remember, I was a research librarian in a former life, so I could even use proper APA citation and all that fancy-ass shit, but then you'd get bored and possibly set this book down, and that won't help you learn to love your body, so just trust me when I say it's fucking good for you.

If you're reading this as an e-book, then you'll probably want to buy yourself a journal to write in. It doesn't have to be fancy. It could just be a notebook. I do advise against using scraps of paper or anything loose-leaf unless you can bind it and keep it together. Why? Because once you get several entries down, you're going to want to go back and re-read what you wrote. I bet after a little bit of time writing down your thoughts and reading this book, you'll be able to see the progress you're making through your journal entries.

If you bought the paperback version of this book, you're golden, because you can just write your journaling portions right here! I will try to give you plenty of space to express yourself, but if you're verbose (like me), feel free to get a notebook so you can really go to town.

Another option you might want to consider is a blog. There are several free websites where you can start one, and just because you're writing it online doesn't mean you have to share it with other people. You can set your privacy to your eyes only, or maybe you want to share it with a small group of like-minded folks. However, consider how empowering it could be for you if others read your words and were inspired by your thoughts. That would be pretty damn awesome, kinda like I'm passing the baton to you!

That said, are you ready for your first assignment? Oh, wait! One more thing—

How to Journal

Most of you are probably not professional writers, and even if you are, journaling is quite a bit different than other types of writing. Some people have a hard time getting their thoughts down on paper, but remember this: writing is essentially the same thing as talking. Pretend you are talking to your closest friend, if that helps. I pretend I'm talking to myself because I do that shit anyway. (All. The. Time.)

I recommend just letting the words flow—not bothering to worry about grammar and spelling or if it's making sense. I'm an editor and self-professed grammar snob, and *I'm* giving you this advice! I know, it's hard for me to believe too, but really, stream-of-consciousness writing works best for journaling. It's because you don't get a chance to censor yourself. You just keep trucking right along, and sometimes things will come out that were so repressed, you might not have even known you were thinking them.

So whether you're typing or writing longhand, crack those knuckles and get to work! Your first assignment is on the very next page.

Journaling Assignment #1: Thinking back...

Think back to the very first time you remember having a negative thought about your body. Maybe someone called you fat or chubby, or they said you needed to lose weight. Maybe you noticed your body was bigger than your peers'. Maybe a friend of yours went on a diet, and it made you look at your own body more critically. How old were you? What was happening in your life at that time? What or who made you have that thought?

Write about that memory and how it made you feel.

K.L. MONTGOMERY

The Misogynistic Myth of Feminine Beauty Standards

Whew, that's a mouthful of a chapter title, isn't it?

Can I tell you something you might not want to hear? I'm probably going to tell you a lot of things you don't want to hear in the course of this book. This won't be the first or last time, but it might be a statement that feels like a slap in the face at first.

Our society's standards of beauty for women were borne out of The Patriarchy.

Don't know what The Patriarchy means? Here's the definition from Wikipedia:

"Patriarchy is a social system in which men hold primary power and predominate in roles of political leadership, moral authority, social privilege and control of property. Some patriarchal societies are also patrilineal, meaning that property and title are inherited by the male lineage."

I'm going to be talking about the historical perspective now, and by historical I mean "recorded" history, because many researchers believe humans had other societal structures in pre-historic times when we were nomadic hunter-gatherers. (For more on that read *Sex at Dawn*, listed in the bibliography at the end of this section. It warms my little librarian heart that I'm offering a bibliography in this book!) In patriarchal societies (*and guess what, that's what ours is*), women are seen as property.

It all started when humans (ahem…the male ones) decided to lay claim to *actual* property: land.

Why stop there? men thought. *We could own lots of other things too: animals, weapons, minerals. But the sky's the limit, right? (Wrong. We can conquer the moon and other planets too if we create the right technology.) But, hey, it would be super cool and make us feel super important if we could own women and children too.*

And then they made it so.

But they didn't want just any old women. They wanted fresh ones. *Virgins.*

Please pardon a little soap-box tangent:

By the way, our entire concept of virginity is a patriarchal social construct. Don't believe me? Answer these questions:

When does a lesbian lose her virginity?

How about a gay man?

How about someone who is intersex?

If you said for lesbians, when they're with a woman for the first time, giving or receiving oral sex; or for gay males, the first time they have anal intercourse, then ask yourself this: why do you consider a straight man or woman who has done oral or anal to still be a virgin because they haven't had vaginal intercourse? It's a crazy, ridiculous inconsistency, don't you think?

Don't think the concept of virginity was designed by men to control and subjugate women? Then why, throughout history, did it never matter if a man was a virgin? Only a woman?

Sorry, about that, I'll step down from my soapbox now. For that issue, anyway.

A lot of the beauty ideals we have that are inextricably linked to youth are also linked to virginity, because, guess what, "virgins" tend to be young. Women who haven't birthed children tend to be slimmer, too. Boom, it was the beginning of slut-shaming, fat-shaming and age discrimination, all because men wanted to be the first one (and preferably *only* one) to put their dicks inside the woman (their property) of their choosing.

For much of recorded history, once a woman had been with a man, she didn't have any value. It's like when you buy a new car, and as soon as you drive it off the lot, it depreciates by several thousand dollars—only worse because women are *people*, not *cars*. Women were a commodity, and their value was based on a) looks, b) virgin status, c) whether their daddies had money or status, and d) whether they could pop out babies. On all counts, it was *men* who decided these were the qualities that mattered.

Tell me that's not completely and horribly sick and twisted.

We are, thousands of years later, *still* trying to eradicate these misogynistic and sexist notions because we now know that women have value beyond beauty, beyond virginity, and beyond motherhood. A woman can be intelligent, strong, and contribute to society and a) never sleep with a man and b) never have children. It took us a LONG time to figure that out, folks. A Long. Fucking. Time. Too long.

Hell, in the U.S., women have only had the right to vote for 100 years! In some countries, women still don't have any rights. But don't get me started on that, or I'll fly off on another tangent like the virginity thing (by the way, the countries where women still don't have any rights are the ones where virgins are still a commodity—that is NOT a coincidence.)

We have all sorts of vestiges of this misogyny hanging around today in our beauty standards. We still slut-shame women who flaunt their sexuality, deviate from monogamy, or enjoy sex before marriage. We still prize youth and slimness. And we still send the message to little girls that their value is based on their appearance.

There is *nothing* wrong with a woman wanting to feel and look beautiful for herself. Not a damn thing wrong with it. I love fashion and makeup and jewelry, and I love looking put-together and "pretty."

However, I do that for ME.

We have to teach little girls—and grown women—that they were not put on this planet to be pretty. We were not created to be playthings or property for men. That. Is. Not. Our. Job.

And once we've been "played with," our value is in no way diminished. We have infinite intrinsic value, and it has *nothing* to do with men. Nothing at all.

Ladies, I need you to internalize that. You might need to tell yourself that over and over again. It's going to be one of those daily affirmations at the end of the book. I'm going to talk about it more when I talk about sex, dating and relationships later on. But I need you to start planting those seeds in your mind right now:

IT IS NOT YOUR JOB TO BE PRETTY.

Here is some further reading on the topic (A Bibliography, YAY!), if you're interested:

The Beauty Myth: How Images of Beauty Are Used Against Women by Naomi Wolf

Sex at Dawn by Christopher Ryan and Cacilda Jetha

Beauty & Misogyny: Harmful Cultural Practices in the West by Sheila Jeffreys

Unbearable Weight: Feminism, Western Culture, and the Body by Susan Bordo

Unladylike: A Field Guide to Smashing the Patriarchy and Claiming Your Space by Cristen Conger and Caroline Ervin

The Purity Myth: How America's Obsession with Virginity Is Hurting Young Women by Jessica Valenti

"Beauty Standards: The Ugliest Trick of Patriarchy" https://feminisminindia.com/2017/05/10/beauty-standards-ugliest-trick/

Time to Get Deprogrammed

There are a number of messages we've received about our bodies since the time we were born. Many of those messages were not meant to harm us, but because our society is obsessed with thinness, youth and beauty (and those three concepts seem to be inextricably linked in society's view), many people don't realize that several of these messages are sizeist, sexist, racist and ableist. And probably other -ists I'm not even thinking of.

Oh, did you see the word *sizeist*?

I'm typing this in Microsoft Word, which doesn't even recognize "sizeist" as a word. I suppose I will have to add it to my dictionary, because I will be using it throughout the book.

You probably know what sexism and racism are, right? Sexism is when you overgeneralize and make assumptions about a person based on their gender, or you discriminate against them on the basis of their gender. Swap out "race" for "gender," and you have a definition of racism.

Sizeism isn't any different. It's when you overgeneralize and make assumptions about a person based on their size, or you discriminate against them based on their size. Think that's not a thing?

Maybe you've heard some of these stereotypes before:

Fat people are lazy.

Fat people are slow or dumb.

Fat people smell bad.

Fat people don't exercise.

Fat people have poor hygiene.

Fat people eat too much.

Fat people are unhealthy.

Fat people only eat junk food.

Those are all examples of overgeneralizations and assumptions based on someone's size. *Oh, okay, sure thing, Krista, but that doesn't mean fat people are discriminated against.*

Oh, yeah? You want me to break out my APA citations?

I could, you know. But the simple truth is that fat people

-are less likely to be hired and promoted

-earn less on average than their thinner peers

-are less likely to get quality medical care compared to their straight-sized peers

-according to some research, fat women are more likely to be convicted of a crime by male jurors than thinner women

-are the victims of countless microaggressions on a daily basis. Microaggressions are somewhat subtle or seemingly innocuous treatment that reminds fat people they have a lower status than smaller people.

Fat people are given the message that they don't deserve to be happy until they lose weight and conform to society's very narrow definition of "normal body size." Very little room is made in society's standards of beauty for people who don't "measure up." It's actually not even just being fat that is an issue in this day and age. It's being the wrong type of fat. I'm about to go on a very short tangent, so strap yourselves in:

There is growing acceptance for a very narrow subset of bigger bodies. For the most part, these bigger bodies are white, cis female, and have an hourglass shape. That's great if you happen to be a curvy white biologically female person. It's not so great if you are a person of color, are a trans woman or your body shape is anything other than hourglass.

My message of body positivity is for *everyone*. It doesn't matter your weight, shape, skin color, gender. I call my book "The Fat Girl's Guide" mostly because I wrote a novel called *Fat Girl*, and in it I talk about how being a Fat Girl is more of a mindset than having to do with your gender or actual weight.

The really damaging part of these messages is that they start when we are so young that they become internalized in our psyches. We come to believe it is our own voice telling us we're not worthy—not the parent or peer or whoever said it.

I have thought a lot about what messages I received when I was growing up. Most of mine came from my mother, but many came from peers, and some came from doctors. Here are some of the verbal and non-verbal messages I received:

-I should cover up my body.

-I shouldn't wear anything too short or too tight or horizontally striped.

-I look best in dresses.

-I can't be popular if I am fat.

-Boys won't like me if I am fat.

-It's okay for people to make fun of me for being fat.

-I'm "less than" because I need to shop in the "plus" department.

-I should choose activities that burn more calories instead of my favorite hobbies of reading and playing the piano (a doctor actually told me that when I was about eleven).

-My sister is more fun to shop for/buy clothes for because she has a thinner, more athletic body.

-I should go on a diet starting at age eleven.

-If I lose X pounds, my mom will reward me.

-I'm fat, so it's okay for people to question my health, my fitness, and how much I eat.

Is it any wonder that I started to develop a major eating disorder when I was fourteen? What is even worse is that my family turned a blind eye to it. No one was even remotely concerned that I didn't eat or that I lost forty pounds in two months. No one asked me if I was starving myself or over-exercising. It was all okay because I finally looked "normal."

I still to this very day carry the weight of all that on my shoulders. Those words and ideas are so deeply embedded in my soul, they've left indelible scars. That pain will *never* go away. As a matter of fact, I'm sitting here at my kitchen table typing this with tears streaming down my damn cheeks because it doesn't matter how much time passes, I will never not cry when I think about those horrible things.

And do you know what's even worse? Many of my readers will have even more heartbreaking stories than I do. My parents loved me—despite my being fat—I know they did and still do. I didn't look the way they wanted me to look, but otherwise, I was not a disappointment. I was smart and an A student; I had friends; had some talents such as singing, writing and playing the piano; and was well-adjusted and all that. But there are plenty of children who do not grow up in loving homes, whose parents outwardly ridicule them and don't use the subtle "microaggression" type behaviors my family employed. You might very well be the grown-up version of one of those children. You might be carrying around a whole host of burdens you've never come to terms with, and what I'm going to ask you to do in the next journaling session might be heart-wrenchingly painful for you.

I still want you to do it, though. And not because I'm a sadist, but because it's part of the work. I warned you this would be a lot of work—the emotionally taxing kind. You kept reading after the first section because you agreed that you wanted to love your body. But first you have to face these demons.

Why?

The title of this chapter is the reason. You have to deprogram yourself.

When you're bombarded with the type of messages I listed above, you cannot help but internalize them. If you hear the same thing over and over, you're bound to believe it.

Maybe you didn't think you deserved to be happy or to be treated like everyone else.

Maybe you thought there were certain foods you shouldn't eat or clothes you shouldn't wear.

Maybe you thought there were places you couldn't go or activities you couldn't participate in.

Maybe you didn't think you were worthy of your family's love, of friendship, of romantic love.

I'm here to tell you that if you internalized any of those ideas from things you heard growing up, THOSE IDEAS ARE PATENTLY FALSE.

It's time to start your deprogramming.

Journaling Assignment #2: Messages

Just like I listed the messages, both verbal and nonverbal, I received growing up about my weight, I want you to do the same. Think about things your parents, siblings, friends, extended family, teachers, doctors, coaches or other adults might have said to you. Think about things your classmates said or did. Chances are pretty good you didn't just decide you were "fat." Someone gave you that idea, or there was something that triggered that idea in your mind. It is probably going to bring up some painful stuff from your past, but it's important to come to terms with the events that shaped your current attitudes. Go on, and I'll be here with a virtual hug when you're done.

THE FAT GIRL'S GUIDE TO LOVING YOUR BODY

Why We Need to Reclaim the Word Fat

First off, big hugs for completing that last journaling assignment. I know it's not easy to think about these things. Like I said in the beginning, you have a lot of hard work ahead of you—and some of it is going to be downright painful. But you've got this! I'm here with you every step of the way.

Okay, so we're going to talk now about why we need to reclaim the word "fat."

I probably should have started off with this, right? It's in the title of the book, after all. Well, first I had to get your trust and gain your interest, because this is super important. Why am I using the word "fat," anyway?

When I published my book *Fat Girl* in 2015, I figured some people would have a problem with the title. Indeed, I received several reviews with negative feedback about the title. But I had a good reason for using it. As a matter of fact, Claire, the main character in the book, goes on a huge diatribe about why "fat" is actually the best and most appropriate word.

I'm a writer. As you probably know, I write romance novels. Most writers love words, and we always diligently try to find the best and most appropriate word for everything. We wouldn't call something merely "big" if it was gargantuan. We wouldn't say someone was "annoying" if the person in question was, in fact, a raging twatwaffle. It's the same thing with "fat." Few words are simpler or more descriptive for someone who has extra adipose tissue than "fat."

We've been told that being "fat" is the worst fate imaginable. But the truth is, we all have some fat on our bodies. Some of us just have more than others. Some of us have more melanin than others. Some of us have more hair. It doesn't fucking matter. How much fat you have isn't any different than how much melanin or hair you have. YOU ARE STILL HUMAN NO MATTER WHAT.

Do you know what we all have exactly the same amount of?

We all have ONE heart.

My point is, there is nothing wrong with the word "fat" other than the fact that society demonizes it. Nothing irritates me more than making a reference to being fat and having someone say, "You're not fat;

you're X" where X can stand for a *euphemism* for fat (curvy, fluffy, thick, etc.) or something like "beautiful" that has absolutely nothing to do with weight in the first place.

When you say, "You're not fat, you're beautiful," you're basically implying the two are mutually exclusive.

And they're not. Oh, my dear, they are most certainly not mutually exclusive. And if you think they are, then read on, because I want to change your mind by the end of this book.

My personal vote is for reclaiming the word. I feel like we should be able to use it with no judgment or value thrust upon it. It's simply a term for adipose tissue, and those of us who are fat have plenty of that.

It's kind of like sexually progressive folks who have reclaimed the word "slut." It's always had a negative connotation, but they are taking it back to be sex positive, denoting someone who embraces their sexuality and their consensual sexual choices. By the way, I'm totally on board with that too.

Oh, and speaking of sex...yes, we'll be talking about that later in the book.

I'll use the term "fat girls" or "fat people" here as a broad category of people who carry more weight than what is commonly considered to be "straight-sized." I also might say "thinner counterparts" to mean those who are considered to have "conventional" or "average"-sized bodies. It's hard to use all of these terms without definitions because not everyone agrees on who is fat, who is overweight, who is obese and who is morbidly obese—isn't that the worst term ever? If you go by the BMI chart (which is a bunch of sexist, racist BS), then much of the population is overweight. We are a nation of Fat Girls, y'all! *snickers*

(Read this for more information on BMI:
https://www.npr.org/templates/story/story.php?storyId=106268439)

As with sexuality and gender, I feel that people should choose their own labels for their bodies. Maybe one woman identifies as a fat girl at a size fourteen. I personally didn't feel like a fat girl at that size, not in the same way I do at my current size. Some other women might not consider themselves fat at size eighteen or twenty. Though some fat acceptance spaces support the notion that a minimum size is required to suffer the effects of fat phobia and stigmatization, in this space (my book and my online Facebook group that accompanies it), I would rather leave it to the individual to decide if the terms describe them.

I'm also going to use the term "body positive" or "bopo" (for short) journey to talk about your progress through the material and journaling assignments presented in this book. I wanted to address the language I'd be using so I can make sure we're all on the same page. *wink*

Have a question about my terminology? Feel free to email me at hello@mountainswanted.com.

Can I Use This Book If I'm Not Fat?

I figured I would get this question sooner or later, so I thought I'd go ahead and address it here toward the beginning after we got a few other important agenda items out of the way. I know that straight-sized/thinner people have hang-ups about their bodies too. That is not solely the sphere of fat girls. When I was on the smaller side of the vast spectrum of weights I've been in my life, I wouldn't have considered myself a fat girl, but, boy, could I have used a book like this back then—especially since I was starving myself and maintaining my smaller size through very unhealthy means.

If you're a smaller person and want to go on this journey so you can love your body, of course that's fine! However, you may not identify with some of the material in the book, like the parts about dealing with body- and fat-shamers, or the medical community, or the extra pressures and feelings surrounding dating, relationships and sex.

There is such a thing called *thin privilege*, and I want you to understand that as you read. Just because you have not experienced the bullying, discrimination, and micro-aggressions that many, many fat people have doesn't mean they don't experience that negativity and those attacks every single day. Be aware that almost everything in the world is catered toward straight-sized folks: clothing, furniture, transportation, entertainment (ever try to squeeze into a seat at a Broadway theater? *Ugh.*) Be aware that fat people face issues that you could probably never dream of.

I would be very curious to know how a straight-sized person feels after completing this book and the journaling assignments, so if you do, please feel free to drop me a line and give me your thoughts. I always love hearing from readers: hello@mountainswanted.com.

What's the difference between Body Positivity and Fat Acceptance?

This is a topic that has already come up a few times in *The Fat Girl's Guide to Loving Your Body* group I started on Facebook (https://www.facebook.com/groups/FGGLYB/). There are a couple of different camps in the pro-fat community, and I'm sorry to report that there is sometimes animosity between them.

Body positivity folks advocate for self-love and loving your body regardless of your size or weight. There's also a subset of that movement that advocates for "health at every size." One of the common mantras you hear from this group is "Every body is a good body." Body positivity also champions diversity in shape, in ability, in skin color, age, etc., fostering the idea that there is beauty in diversity, and beauty need not conform to outdated standards (i.e. the ones that arose from the patriarchy, like we discussed earlier).

Fat positivity, fat acceptance, and fat liberation folks look at it from more of a human rights angle and focus exclusively on fat bodies. They advocate for equality for fat people. Like we saw earlier, there are many ways in which fat people are marginalized in our society, and it has always been acceptable to treat those with bigger bodies differently than straight-sized folks. Fat acceptance raises awareness about the ways in which fat bodies are marginalized and discriminated against and teaches the concept of "thin privilege." Thin privilege encompasses advantages that thin people have in society without even knowing it. For example, thinner people are catered to by clothing designers, furniture designers, car and airplane engineers, and so on. They are more likely to receive adequate health care and get hired and promoted at their jobs.

So as you can see, each movement has a different focus. Often I see bickering between people from both camps, and it really frustrates me. I don't think you have to be strictly one or the other. You can believe everyone has a right to feel good and happy about their bodies AND feel that fat people deserve the same basic human rights as other people.

The problem is, like I mentioned before, some so-called body positive folks seem to be jumping on the bandwagon because it's a trendy hashtag, but they are really only supporting white, cis female, hourglass-shaped bodies.

As you might imagine, that drives a lot of the other, true bopo folks nutso. And rightfully so.

I see value in both causes and a need for both movements. Body positivity *should* be for everyone—because, as the mantra goes, *every body IS a good body*. At the same time, fat people are harassed, shamed, bullied and discriminated against (as we talked about before) and that needs to change *pronto allegro*.

I hope people in both camps can find common ground because I think those of us who have a real passion and heart for these ideals can work together to bring about positive change in our world. And I'm trying to do my part with this book.

Your Relationship With Food

There's a lot more involved in having a larger body than just one's diet, but we can't ignore the challenges we face just in the simple and life-sustaining act of eating. Sustenance can be a battleground for a fat person. Don't think you have food issues? How many of these questions can you answer yes to?

Have you ever been on a diet?

Have you ever binged on food?

Have you ever tried to limit a certain kind of food, i.e. carbs, sugars, fats, etc.?

Have you ever fasted?

Do you think of foods as being either good or bad?

Do you avoid eating any foods because you are afraid they will make you gain weight?

Have you ever eaten foods you didn't enjoy because you thought they would help you lose weight?

Have you ever tracked your calories and/or macronutrients?

Have you ever punished yourself by not letting yourself eat something you want?

Have you ever punished yourself for eating something you didn't think you should eat by either starving yourself to make up for the calories or forcing yourself to burn them off through exercise?

Have you ever rewarded yourself with food?

Let me ask you to reflect upon something else. Every species on the planet has to eat to live. But I don't know of any other species that purposely limit their food intake in order to lose weight. Wild animals typically are not fat. Animals don't seem to accumulate excess weight until their food is controlled by humans.

So why is something that should be so simple, so basic, so primal even—why is it so damn hard?

I'm not going to go into a lot of science here, but I think it's pretty evident that the human diet has evolved a great deal over time, and probably the most radical period of change is the one we are living in now. If you think about the way diets have changed in the past one hundred years, you will see that we've gone from eating foods produced by nature to foods with tons of chemicals in them. Hell, you can't even pronounce some of the ingredients in the foods we eat these days.

That's not even getting into the socioeconomic factors that impact obesity, food quality and availability. The healthiest foods are the most expensive. Is it any wonder that lower-income folks have a tendency to be fatter than those with higher incomes?

The change in ingredients and how food is manufactured along with the cheapness of ingredients such as corn syrup have led to the development of some pretty serious food hang-ups. Never before has there been so much "junk food" so cheaply and readily available. And not just a choice between cookies or cake or pie, but the choice between thousands of types of cookies, cakes, and pies.

We've assigned moral values to food. We herald "good," healthy foods as our saviors, the foods that are going to make us thin. We feel like saints when we eat broccoli, cauliflower, kale, so-called "superfoods" and the like.

On the other hand, we demonize foods we're afraid will make us fat. Anything with refined flours or sugars, anything with carbs or the wrong kind of fats. If we can overcome temptation by these foods, it's like we're freakin' Joan of Arc or something.

Has anyone ever noticed what happens when we label something as "bad"? Things that might corrupt our bodies or our minds? Sex, drugs, alcohol, cigarettes, and potato chips, right? Things we just can't seem to get enough of. Things we become addicted to. And the more we vilify these things, the more we want them.

Does anyone see a problem with that when it comes to food—the thing we don't have a choice but to consume? Eating food is like breathing oxygen. Without either, we'd die.

We spend so much of our energy restricting "bad" foods that we give them way too much power. Why do you think we binge eat? We binge because we feel like we shouldn't be eating those things in the first place. And once we start, we've already had a moral failing—so we might as well continue to binge.

One of the things I'd like you to do from here on out is to stop assigning moral values to food. Try not to think of them as bad or good. I know it's very hard to do because it's been beaten into us, drilled into our brains so deep it's hard to forget. But trust me when I say it is not a productive mentality. It is actually extremely counterproductive.

I've been practicing something for the past few years called intuitive eating. It's so simple and natural, it ought to just be called "eating." It's basically where you eat when you're hungry and don't eat when you aren't. And you eat whatever you want when you're hungry, what your body is telling you it craves. It's been interesting to me because I've found I have a very distinct pattern that actually falls in line with the intermittent fasting diet. I don't advocate fasting by any means—not forcing yourself to fast, anyway—but when I eat intuitively, that's essentially what ends up happening. I don't eat breakfast except for coffee. I just don't feel like eating in the morning. I don't usually get hungry till ten o'clock or later. Almost all my meals and snacks fall between ten AM and six PM. I don't typically eat after six, whereas before I started intuitive eating, I often snacked at night—usually because I'd starved myself all day and was too hungry not to. But when I listen to my body, my hunger seems to turn off after dinner and then stays at bay till late the next morning.

If you decide to practice intuitive eating, you may discover what I did: you eat a lot less when you give yourself permission to eat whatever you want, whenever you want. Do you know what else is great about it? You don't have to feel guilty or bad for eating so-called "bad" foods. And you're much less likely to crave the "bad" foods because you don't consider them "bad" anymore, and you grant yourself permission to eat them.

This major epiphany is coming from the woman who counted every damn calorie and tracked them off and on for years and years. Decades, even. Intuitive eating could not be further from what I have practiced for most of my life. I guess that makes my former status quo "counter-intuitive eating."

So, I bet you are all wondering if I have gained or lost weight doing intuitive eating.

This is where I stomp my foot and scream at the top of my lungs: "IT DOESN'T MATTER!"

But why doesn't it matter? Am I just going to get fatter if I eat whatever I want whenever I want?

Doesn't that mean I can just camp out on my couch and subsist on a diet of Doritos and Fudge Rounds?

Well, yeah, I suppose you could. But I would venture if you did do that, then you haven't completed the step of removing the moral value you assign to food. Because if you no longer divide foods into good or bad, I can almost guarantee you that your balance of healthier, more nutritionally dense foods versus higher-calorie, less nutritionally dense foods will improve. When you take away the taboo, foods like Doritos and Fudge Rounds will probably lose their appeal.

Will you still want cheesecake? Yes, you will. I can promise you that.

But you will probably eat one slice, feel zero guilt, and get on with your life.

Instead of taking a bite, feeling guilty, so you take another bite, and then another, and then the next thing you know you've become a shark at a feeding frenzy and the whole damn cheesecake has vanished into thin air (spoiler alert: it's in your belly.)

So, what do you think? Will this be a hard change for you to make?

You can explore your feelings surrounding food in the next journaling assignment, which is, you guessed it, on the next page!

Happy writing!

Journaling Assignment #3: Tell Me About Your Mother, I Mean, Your Relationship with Food

I polled the readers in my Facebook group I created specifically for this book about when they went on their first diet. The answers I received ranged from eight to twenty years old, with the majority falling between the ages of ten and fourteen. I know my first diet was at ten or eleven, so these answers were not even shocking to me. But they *are* disheartening. Just when we were establishing a healthy relationship with food, we went on (or were forced to go on) a diet. No wonder we are screwed up, you know?

What is your relationship with food like? Do you divide foods into good and bad? How will you go about changing your mentality around food to make it easier for you to love your body?

THE FAT GIRL'S GUIDE TO LOVING YOUR BODY

What is Diet Culture and Why Is It So Harmful?

First off, let me hit you upside the head with a figure, okay?

My sources say that the U.S. weight loss industry is worth 72 billion dollars in 2019—even though the number of dieters is down thanks to the body positive and fat acceptance movements. (bit.ly/FGGLink1)

So even though people like me are over here shouting our freaking heads off about body positivity, we're still spending an absolutely insane amount of money on weight loss drugs, pills, potions, programs, and false promises.

Why is that, exactly?

Because of our obsession with losing weight.

And we are downright OBSESSED with it.

What is one of the highest compliments you can pay someone?

"Hey, have you lost weight?"

Given the choice of being thin or rich for the rest of your life, many women would choose being thin. Or they'd pick being rich so they could hire personal trainers and a chef, or pay for plastic surgery—thereby attaining thinness in addition to wealth. *Sneaky bitches, huh?*

Diet culture is a system of beliefs that equates thinness with virtue and fat with vice. Thinness is worshipped, while fatness is considered a moral failing. Remember when we talked about "good" foods and "bad" foods? That mindset is a big component of diet culture, but diet culture extends even further by projecting moral judgment onto actual people, not just food.

Have you ever heard someone decline dessert with the excuse, "I promised myself I'd be *good* tonight"?

Do not mistake the language: we feel *virtuous* and *saintly* when we deny ourselves food. We feel *sinful* and *naughty* when we indulge ourselves.

This mindset is doing us a giant disservice—and it's not hard to see the proof of it. Are people getting thinner over time? *Hell to the no.* Our society keeps getting fatter and fatter. We don't even blink an eye when we hear "obesity epidemic" anymore because we hear it ALL the time. Clearly, diet culture is NOT working. It's costing us money, health, and happiness—and time. And it's making some assholes really fucking rich. Who do you think benefits when a diet craze sweeps the nation? *Hint: it's not the dieters.* Who invented Keto, anyway? (That happens to be the diet craze du jour as I write this, but I'm sure it will be replaced by something else soon.) The person who invented and/or popularized Keto plus lots of others who sell its products and services have no doubt capitalized on its success.

But what about the people who have actually been on that diet? From what I understand, as soon as you go off it, you gain the weight back. And it's not like you get a refund on any pills, potions, books, videos, apps or other propaganda you've purchased. So you might end up fat again, but the Keto propagandists are still rollin' in dough.

Furthermore, how can a diet be touted as so incredible and effective—or be endorsed by medical professionals—if you can NEVER go off it? If it's not in the least bit sustainable? If it involves putting your body into a harmful, unnatural state to even work?

There is nothing evil about sugar. There is nothing devilish about carbs. Kale is not endorsed by God, okay? Angels do not sing when you eat quinoa, I promise. They are all just foods. Some may have more nutritional value than others, but what you eat does NOT make you good or bad.

Let's get back to that compliment I mentioned just a moment ago:

Have you lost weight?

The only compliment in our language that might possibly be more flattering is "You look younger than your age."

Do you ask someone you haven't seen in a while if they have *gained* weight? No, not unless you are a very rude, unkind person. So why do we believe it's okay to ask if someone has lost weight?

Did you know there are other reasons for weight loss other than going on an elective diet? Here are a few of them:

- Surgery
- Depression
- Illness
- Drugs (both prescription and illicit)

For the most part, I don't think people would want to celebrate those things. So why do we always assume if someone has lost weight that they a) tried to and b) wanted to?

It's a horrible assumption. It's a dangerous assumption.

It's especially dangerous when someone has an eating disorder and is fueled by those sorts of "compliments." I know this firsthand from when I was starving myself. Even negative reactions to weight loss can fuel eating disorders. Once, after my second son was born and I'd lost over a hundred pounds, someone told me I looked sick, and they actually asked me if I had cancer. I was not even offended. It only reaffirmed what I had been doing, which was eating 300-600 calories a day and burning three to four times that with exercise.

Another thing that really fuels diet culture and the moral judgment of weight is when people use social media to celebrate their weight loss or chronicle their "weight loss journeys."

Just a note about purposely trying to lose weight while still loving your body: I'm going to cover this in a different section of the book. I've struggled with reconciling the whole body positive thing and still wanting to be smaller/fitter/healthier, and to be honest, I'm still working on it. But I think there is a right way and a wrong way to go about it. I will be talking about that in a different chapter, so stay tuned.

How many times have you seen friends post on social media: "I'm down another dress size!" or "I lost ten pounds!" or "I only need to lose five more pounds to get to my goal weight."

It might seem innocuous, but it can be very triggering to people who struggle with their weight. Even if you want to be happy for your friend, sometimes it can be impossible to harness your feelings of jealousy when you see posts like that. Your friend is also sending the message that there was something wrong with her body before, and now her body is better. If you are heavier than your friend, it can feel like a form of fat shaming, especially if your friend carries on about how fat/disgusting/unattractive their former body was.

I understand why people do it: it provides a sense of accountability, and people gobble up the positive feedback (pardon the pun). But this type of affirmation for weight loss coupled with posts lamenting weight gain only fuel diet culture. And what happens when these people (almost inevitably) gain the weight back? I don't see anyone bragging about that on social media. Instead, they are steeped in shame and feelings of failure, which they must bear in private. Later when I talk about your media diet, all the social media, television, news, and movies you consume, we will revisit this topic.

So, if after reading this, you're still skeptical about the damaging effects of diet culture, let me just issue you a challenge going forward, alright?

Keep your eyes and ears open for the messages all around you pertaining to weight loss, dieting, and body size.

Is what they're selling *healthy*? By healthy, I mean *mentally* as well as physically.

Is what they're selling *sustainable*?

Will what they're selling help you truly learn to love and accept your body no matter what size it is?

Meet Your New Body

Okay, so you aren't literally getting a new body. Figured I better put that out there in case any of you try to sue me for false advertising or something. Your body won't be new, but the way you look at it will be. So, in a way, it will be your mind that's new, not your body.

There is an incredible amount of pressure on women to have a certain type of body. Some of us had that so-called "ideal body" at some point in our lives, whereas others of us never have. Despite some voices from diet culture yelling very loudly that "everyone can have the body you've always dreamed of if you just follow X or buy Y or do Z!" it's simply not true. Some researchers estimate that your genes are 80% responsible for determining your weight and body shape.

One thing I learned when I lost all the weight those times I was starving myself and over-exercising is that I still couldn't attain society's idea of the perfect body. My hips were too wide. My thighs were too thick. I would never look like a Victoria's Secret model no matter how much weight I lost. I'm just not built that way. Thanks, Mom and Dad, I'm pretty sure you're to blame for that! (Okay, at least 80% to blame!)

Society's ideal is simply *not possible* for everyone. We are all shaped differently. Some of us are short-waisted, some long-waisted. Some of us are tall, some short. Some of us have ample boobage, and some of us have flatter chests. Some of us have big, round butts, and some of us have smaller, flatter butts. Some of us have large frames, and some small.

WE ALL LOOK DIFFERENT! And that is an incredible, glorious thing.

I have no interest in society being a huge mass of clones, do you? If you're a Star Wars fan, you remember that movie *Attack of the Clones*, and it sucked, right? Not even just the clone part of it, but the entire damn movie. But I digress…

So this ideal that's thrust in our faces in a million different ways—in the form of models, actresses, singers, and public figures all over the world—the ideal that's dangled like a carrot in front of us our entire lives isn't even possible, not even *remotely* attainable, for a large percentage of the population!

Basically, it's a Big. Fat. Hairy. Lie.

We're going to talk more about media and representation later in the book, but let me tell you about something that had a profound impact on me. But first, a little background.

We have been fed a steady diet of this so-called "perfect body" for our entire lives. Think about all of the media you've been exposed to since the time you were a small child. Think about every woman you saw in the movies, on television, in magazine ads, on billboards, on product packaging, in commercials, modeling clothing, broadcasting the news. What did these women's bodies look like?

I'm willing to bet that 99% of the women you saw in these capacities had a thin, or at least a straight-sized body, and a high percentage of them had the "perfect" body or close to a "perfect" body.

Minority and marginalized populations have been screaming for decades that they need more and better representation in media. Why? Because when you don't see anyone who looks like you in all of the places I mentioned above, you start to wonder what's wrong with yourself. If the women in the above capacities are what's normal, then what are you?

It's the same principle behind bringing awareness to women in STEM fields, for example. Because little girls who don't see female engineers, doctors, computer programmers, mathematicians, physicists, chemists, etc. might not see those careers as possible or viable for themselves. Representation matters. A LOT.

When you've been fed a steady diet of so-called "perfect" bodies your entire life, how would you not come to believe there is something wrong with YOUR body?

I don't think I realized the dire lack of representation of plus-sized models and actresses until I began following lots of body positive accounts on Instagram, and until I started shopping at Torrid. For the first time, I was seeing bigger and fatter bodies existing like normal humans. They were modeling clothes; they were having families, working in careers, showing they exist right alongside all the "perfect" bodies crammed down our throats day in and day out for years and years.

But let me tell you about the moment it really, truly hit home for me.

Did you see the show *Shrill* with Aidy Bryant on Hulu earlier this year? I have loved Aidy Bryant on *Saturday Night Live* forever now, and when I saw the trailer for this show, I was excited but also a bit trepidatious. I loved the idea of a fat woman finally getting to be the heroine in a show—not the sidekick or best friend, but the actual honest-to-god main character. Almost all of the heroines in my romance novels are plus-sized chicks, and there is some pretty good plus-size rep in indie-published romance novels in general, but let's face it, there aren't too many plus-size actresses getting lead roles YET (at least I hope it's a YET).

What I didn't want to see is a plus-sized woman who was pressured to lose weight and who was miserable with herself and didn't think she deserved to be happy until she lost weight. What I *really* did not want to see is a plus-sized character who didn't think she could date until she lost a few pounds. That kind of bullshit just infuriates me.

So I was thrilled to see that the representation in *Shrill* was fantastic. Does Annie face discrimination and mistreatment because she's fat? Yes, she does, and that part is heartbreakingly realistic. But what was amazing is that she has this fantastic support system—her best friend and roommate is an absolute joy. And at one point, Annie goes to this Fat Babe pool party with her roommate…

Imagine this:

The camera pans across this huge, lush pool, and it's filled with beautiful, laughing and smiling, unapologetic and unashamed fat ladies.

And I sat there watching it, realizing that for the very first time in my entire life I was seeing a whole screen of gorgeous, diverse, plus-sized women who were being portrayed as happy and carefree—and beautiful!

I literally burst into tears. Hell, I'm tearing up just writing this because I remember how absolutely groundbreaking it felt to be watching that moment unfold before me.

My husband was like, "What is your deal? Are you okay?"

And I just sat there, speechless, taking it all in. I tried to explain to him why it had such an impact on me, but I'm not sure he could ever relate. Maybe if he saw an entire screen full of handsome, beefy Italian guys like himself…

Oh, wait, that's been done. Like a million times over.

Beautiful, happy, plus-sized women frolicking in a pool on my screen?

Yeah, never seen that before.

Representation matters. It matters so much. Seeing yourself, seeing people who look like you on TV, in movies, in advertisements—it really, *really* matters.

We're going to talk more about how to fill your diet with body positive inspiration (I like to call it #bopoinspo for short), but in the meantime, we're going to focus on some other things you can do to help reframe the way you see your body.

A Quick Note About Body Dysmorphic Disorder

I just wanted to put this out here because it's an actual psychological disorder characterized by perceiving your body or a part of your body in a way that is not in line with reality. Their scrutiny of their body or body part becomes so profound that it causes anxiety and/or depression. Sufferers may avoid social situations and their relationships may be affected as well.

You can read more about this disorder here: bit.ly/FGGLink2

If you think you might have symptoms of BDD, please talk to your doctor or mental health professional about it.

The next section of this book is about reacquainting yourself with your body and hopefully seeing it in a new light. Remember this isn't about changing your body—it's about changing your mind.

Journal Assignment #4: Photo-Journaling

Can I recommend something to try as you work through this process?

You're probably not going to like the suggestion, but please hear me out. I think it helps with skewed perceptions of our size, and also offers a different perspective when we're used to only seeing ourselves in a mirror all the time.

Willingly be the subject of photographs.

Yeah, I know. Most of us don't like to be in front of the camera, but you promised to be open-minded. (Well, you implied you were going to be when you kept reading this book after the introduction. *wink* It's a technicality maybe, but one I plan on fully leveraging!)

Maybe start with selfies. You don't have to show the photos to anyone, but I think it helps if you do. Try on some different outfits, ones that make you feel happy and beautiful, and snap away. Experiment with angles, with lighting, with makeup if you want. Take some without any makeup. Take full-length photos. Take photos of your face. Take photos of specific body parts.

Ready to take it up a level? Take photos in less clothing. In a swimsuit, or a bra and panties. Really want to be brave? Take a fully nude selfie in the mirror or in the bathtub, whatever floats your boat.

The more photos you take of yourself, I'm guessing that a) the better you will get at creating photos you like and b) the better you will feel about your body. It may take some time. It may feel silly at first. But trust me on this, it really helps. It helps me anyway. I've been doing this for years now.

You can also start an Instagram account and post your photos there. If you don't want to reveal your identity, blur your face or crop it out. Create a handle. Tag your photo with #bodypositive or #fatfashion or one of dozens of bopo hashtags and watch the compliments pour in. Ignore the creepy guys though, and block anyone who sends you a dick pic. It'll happen eventually, with just about as much certainty as ants inviting themselves to a picnic.

Ready to graduate to the next level?

Get someone else to take your photos. Try different settings and clothing changes. Pose or don't pose. I am willing to bet that many of you have not had photos taken of yourself in years. You may purposely avoid being in photos.

Really want to level up? Schedule a boudoir shoot with a professional photographer. Think that's the scariest thing ever? It *is* scary. I've done it before. But trust me on this: I have known a lot of women who've done a boudoir shoot, and I have yet to hear any of them voice regret for doing so.

Sometimes fat people say they feel invisible. I have often felt this way myself. I have actually pondered, "How can I take up so much space and not be seen?"

So take up space. Be seen. Flirt with the camera. Show your smile. Be happy! Capture yourself living your best life. It may be hard to look at those photos, but JUST. DO. IT. Go Nike on it, girls. Prove to the haters and fatphobics that you have just as much right to exist and just as much right to be happy as they do.

Then set all those photos aside—because I want you to bring them back out again when you complete all the tasks in this book. When you've read every word and when you've completed all the assignments, revisit the photos you took, and I bet you'll see yourself in a new light.

But it won't be the photos that are different. It won't be your body that's different. It will be YOU who is different. Different on the inside.

Let's Start at the Bottom and Work Our Way Up

This section of the book is focused on reacquainting yourself with your own body. I know, it sounds ridiculous, but I'm encouraging you to closely examine each part of yourself. You may think you know your body intimately, but I've found that people who have been body-shamed tend to disconnect or disassociate themselves from their bodies or parts of their bodies. You can't love your body if you don't even know it.

Each section will be dedicated to a different region of your body. I want you to write a letter to the body part—yeah, like I said, it sounds ridiculous, but please just trust that there's a method to my madness here, alright? Start with what you've always thought and felt toward that part of your body. Is it a body part you've loved or hated? Why? List all the negative things you've thought and felt about it.

Then I want you to think about all the *good* things about that body part. How does it help you live? How does it contribute to your overall health and wellness? What are some positive points about the way it looks and functions?

Finally, I want you to make a promise to that body part that you'll try your hardest to focus on the positive things you wrote instead of the negative. When you're feeling down about your body, you can come back to that passage in your journal or blog and refresh your memory about the promise you've made.

We're going to start with our feet and legs. Like I said, we're starting at the bottom and working our way up—a very smart way to do things in general, don't you think?

What are some of the horrible things we say about our lower extremities? We might say our feet are too big, too wide, too bony, not bony enough. We may say we have cankles. We may think our feet are ugly. We may hate our calves for being too big or too skinny or not defined enough. Thighs are often a huge source of angst for women (I know mine were for me!) Maybe you think yours are too thick or too thin. I don't know if I've ever heard a woman say she has perfect thighs, have you?

Perhaps your beef with your lower extremities is your skin. Maybe you have cellulite or stretch marks or varicose veins. Maybe the skin isn't smooth or you have scars. Perhaps you just hate shaving your legs and hate that your hair is thick, prickly, and grows too fast.

Those are all things you might hate about your feet and legs. Be thinking about what you might include in your letter because you're going to get a chance to write it very shortly. I know this whole process might sound silly. But just to prove I can walk the walk just like I talk the talk (see what I did there?), I'm going to show you my own letter:

Dear Feet and Legs,

I've never had a big problem with you, Feet. You're pretty decent as far as feet go, except for the occasional flare-up of plantar fasciitis, and wearing a size ten shoe is no fun sometimes. But Legs, you've been a sore spot for me for a long time.

Legs, you are disproportionately large, and that's putting it nicely. I mean, I'm a pretty big-boned person in general, but my thighs are ginormous. *I remember back when I was in the height of my eating disorder days and I used to measure my thighs along with all the other measurements I took. My thighs averaged only about two to three inches less than my waist, meaning they were well over twenty inches around. My calves are also big, and not in a muscular, defined way.*

Because of your size, Legs, I've never been very comfortable wearing shorts, short skirts, or short dresses. I've always felt the need to cover you up—and I have been told I look better if I cover you up. I have loathed the skin you're in, Thighs. You are dimpled with cellulite, and you have been most of my life, even when I was on the thinner side of the spectrum.

I have vilified you, shamed you, covered you, hated you and been embarrassed by you. I've put creams on you, done ridiculous exercises, and god knows what else to try to change the way you look. I've apologized for the space you take up.

I'm not going to do that anymore; I'll be turning over a new leaf. Feet, I'm going to take care of you and not force you into uncomfortable shoes just for the sake of fashion or vanity. You take me where I need to go, and I cannot tell you how much I appreciate that because I love going places. Legs, I'm no longer ashamed of you. I will wear leggings and short dresses and whatever else I desire because my legs are one of the most important parts of me—they don't deserve to be covered up. I owe my mobility to my legs. The fact that I can walk and climb, hike and swim. All of that is possible due to my legs.

My legs are just as good as anyone else's legs. Better even, because they are MINE. They are the only legs I will ever have. These feet are the only feet I will ever have. I will take care of them and cherish them because they have always treated me well and gotten me where I need to go. When they hurt, I will slow down and take care of them. I need you guys to last me another several decades. Just think of all the places we will go together in the future. I can't wait!

I love you, Legs and Feet. Thanks for all you do!

Journaling Assignment #5: Feet & Legs

Write a letter to your feet and legs. Start by apologizing for the negative thoughts or feelings you've had about them throughout your life. Then find some positive things to say and promise them you'll try your hardest to focus on the positive from now on.

THE FAT GIRL'S GUIDE TO LOVING YOUR BODY

I Like Big Butts and I Cannot Lie

When I was growing up, my butt was one part of my body I didn't think that much about—probably helped that I couldn't actually see it. It wasn't until I was in junior high and I tried to squeeze it into Guess jeans (which were all the rage) that I figured out it is big. Really big. I had to buy the biggest size of Guess jeans they made to fit my butt, and then the waist was huge and gapping. But I still insisted on wearing them because…peer pressure. *Sigh*.

I managed to get through the late eighties and early nineties when waify models were en vogue. Obviously, I was more Anna Nicole Smith than Kate Moss. Do you guys actually remember these people or are you more like, wow, this lady is O.L.D. as dirt?

But then something changed a decade or so ago, I guess when JLo, Beyoncé and Kim Kardashian became famous. Big ol' curvy butts were finally en vogue. Yay for me! Maybe Sir Mix A Lot and his iconic "Baby Got Back" song had something to do with it too, I don't know.

(An aside: if you want to look at what body types were fashionable throughout history, this article gives a pretty succinct synopsis: bit.ly/FGGLink3)

Finally, I had a body part that was big, and it was actually socially acceptable for it to be big. But I'm guessing lots of ladies with smaller or flatter derrieres are like, "whoa, now I have a whole new flaw to obsess over." No matter how the pendulum swings, there are "winners" and "losers."

The truth is that body shapes go in and out of style, just like fashion. Actually, it has a lot to do with fashion. The body type that looks best in the fashion trends of the day is the one that rises to the top—but it's always temporary, so that is usually a good thing. So in the eighties when physical fitness and aerobics became popular, and clothes were structured with big shoulder pads, model's bodies followed suit with bigger shoulders, more toned muscles, and more athletic-looking curves. When grunge fashion was trendy in the nineties, that's when waify models gained popularity. In the 2000s, we have had a bit of a return to a curvier physique, but there's still a huge emphasis on thinness. I'm personally waiting for Rubenesque figures to come back en vogue, but I'll probably never see that one make the rounds in my lifetime!

For our next assignment, I'm going to ask you to think about your rear-end. It may seem ass-backwards, but we can really have a lot of hang-ups about this body part that has gained so much attention as of late. You might think yours is too big, too small, too flat, too round, not toned enough, or that the skin is dimpled or stretched or lumpy or whatever. Be thinking of what you want to say to your booty, because it's just about that time…

Journaling Assignment #6: Doin' the Butt

As opposed to "do it in the butt" like Leon Phelps, the Ladies' Man from *Saturday Night Live,* would say. Yeah, that's a totally different advice book. (I'm sure none of you appreciate my silly sense of humor, but whatevs. I'm about to make you write a letter to your butt, so who's the real winner here?)

Write a letter to your backside. Start by apologizing for the ways you might have ridiculed it through the years. Then find some positive things to say before vowing to focus on those positive things in the future!

THE FAT GIRL'S GUIDE TO LOVING YOUR BODY

Waist, Abdomen, and Hips

It's time to head around to the other side of your body and take a gander at your mid-section. There aren't too many body parts more closely associated with fatness than one's waist, am I right? A lot of people carry extra weight around their midsection, even people who are smaller in other places. And we have a lot of insecurities and self-hate tied up in this part of our bodies.

Throughout the history of humankind, a woman's waist has often been the focal point of feminine beauty. Though hips and bottoms fluctuate from smaller to bigger in popularity, it's always been in fashion for women to have small waists. Think about how many years of fashion involved women wearing corsets to make their waists as small as possible—women's internal organs were even rearranged in the process. Some have theorized that from an evolutionary standpoint, if a man meets a woman sporting a tiny waist, chances are pretty good she isn't already knocked up, so perhaps he could do the honors if he so desired. Pretty misogynistic, huh?

Women's waists, bellies and hips tend to spread after childbirth, so that ties in with our obsession with youth that is inextricably linked to societal standards of beauty. It's easy to see how we would fixate on our midsections when nearly every representation of female beauty we've been exposed to features women with relatively slim hips, even narrower waists, and flat bellies.

There's actually a great amount of diversity in women's torsos. Some women are short-waisted, and some are long. Some have slim hips and fuller waists; others have fuller hips and slimmer waists. Some bellies are flat; some have visible abdominal muscles; some have rolls and folds. Some women have stretch marks, and some have scars from c-sections or other surgeries.

The size of your waist does not dictate your femininity, nor does it have anything to do with your worth as a human being.

I think corsets are beautiful from a fashion standpoint. And I understand the hourglass silhouette is a rather aesthetically pleasing one. But if that is not your body shape, you are not any less of a woman.

If your concern is more about your hips or belly, rest assured you're in good company. Most women have lamented the size of their hips and their abdomens at some time or another. Maybe your issue is that you have stretch marks on your skin, either from gaining or losing weight rapidly, or from carrying a baby.

No matter how you got them, it's perfectly normal to have stretch marks. Imagine how much money the beauty industry has made preying on women's insecurities when it comes to stretch marks! It's practically criminal. Especially since it's much more common to have them than not have them. I've had some of my stretch marks since I was a child! And then, when I carried three bouncing baby boys to term (past full term with my firstborn—he really did not want to come out), I got a brand-new batch of stretch marks, and they're not going anywhere twenty-some years later.

Maybe you have an "apron" of fat or loose skin that hangs between your navel and pubic area. I know I do. This can be a real source of grief and self-loathing for some women, but believe me when I say it doesn't have to be. And it doesn't mean you can't be beautiful or you can't wear certain clothes. We'll talk about fat fashion later, but trust me, it is possible to come to terms with this part of your body, even if you don't love it.

You may be thinking, sorry, lady, but I will never love my stomach. When I titled my book *The Fat Girl's Guide to Loving Your Body*, I knew a lot of people were going to say it was impossible because of this part or that. And I know it seems counterintuitive that we're dissecting our bodies into parts for this exercise, but there is a method to my madness. I want you to come to terms with these negative thoughts and feelings you have toward your thighs or hips or bellies or breasts so in the end you can say, you know what? I'm more than just the sum of my parts. My body is a WHOLE body; it's not a puzzle of disconnected pieces.

You may never be 100% in love with your stretch marks or sagging skin.

You may never want to show off your booty.

But you can learn to come to terms with your body parts and work on loving your body as a whole. That's what these journaling assignments are about.

So without further ado, let's move on to the next one, shall we?

Journaling Assignment #7: Waist, Belly & Hips

Like I said, we have a lot riding on this area of our body, especially when it comes to ideals of feminine beauty. Write a letter to your mid-section and apologize for all the negative things you've thought and felt through the years. Then talk about the positive things about this region of your body. Maybe your belly was home to your beautiful children when you were growing them. Or maybe you have wide, feminine hips. Or maybe you just want to celebrate the fact that your hips give you mobility. Seriously, imagine what it would be like to try to move around if you didn't have hips. You'd probably look like a robot! You don't want to look like a robot, right?

…

Arms, Shoulders & Back

It might seem weird that I'm lumping these parts together, but they are kinda connected (see what I did there?) And you may not have as many negative thoughts tied up in your arms, shoulders, and back as other body parts, but I think these parts may be overlooked sources of angst for some women.

Let's start with arms: the traditional feminine ideal is to have long, slim arms. So if yours are thick or muscular, you might not like the way they look. It's more accepted now for women to have muscular arms, but they are still supposed to be thin. It sounds like an oxymoron because it is! It's a little ridiculous to think that women should be thin and at the same time muscular. But that's what society tells us. It's the same mentality that says we should be slim and not have hardly any fat on our bodies, but we should also have big boobs (yup, that will be the next section!)

Or maybe your arms are super skinny and bony? Maybe you're not particularly down with that either. My point is there is a lot of diversity in how actual arms look, yet it's only one shape/size acceptable in our fucked-up beauty standards.

Shoulders are another body part that has clear gender expectations. Women are supposed to have narrow, rounded shoulders, and men are supposed to have broad, strong shoulders, right? So what if you're a chick and you have big shoulders? Well, it doesn't make you any less of a woman, but it may be something you've had to come to terms with—or maybe you're still working on it.

Your back is another body part that you might not think that much about. But society tries to tell us there's a right way to have a back too! (Spoiler alert: there's no wrong way to have a back!) Maybe you have back fat or rolls, or maybe you have hair on your back, I don't know. My point is that your back is strong and can obviously carry a lot of both actual and metaphorical weight, so you should appreciate the shit out of it. Also, it can hurt a LOT when it's injured. I've thrown my back out enough times to know this is one body part you should be extra kind to.

Taken together, these parts of your body are pretty damn important. You wouldn't be much of a human without a spine, am I right? And though you might often wish you had an extra arm/hand, the two you have are probably pretty damn helpful. There may be someone reading this who is missing an arm, so let it be stated unequivocally here that your value has nothing to do with how many arms you have. (You hear that, octopuses?)

Journaling Assignment #8: Arms, Shoulders & Back

I bet you never thought when you bought this book that you'd be writing a letter to your arms, shoulders, and back, but here you are! And here is my maniacal cackling that I've gotten you to do it! Bwahahaha!

Talk about any negative feelings you've had about these parts of your body, along with a heartfelt apology for them, then list some positive attributes about the way they work or look. Finally, promise these mega-important parts you will be as kind as possible and beg them to keep functioning properly for as long as possible. (They may even accept bribes!)

Boobs: You Knew This Was Coming

No part of a woman's body is more tied to notions of femininity than breasts. And fewer body parts have more or more colorful nicknames. No matter if you call them breasts, boobs, tatas, knockers, your rack, tits, the girls or whatever other creative monikers you may have devised, you probably have a lot of feelings wrapped up in those babies.

I've always been well-endowed (well, since I was eleven or twelve). Most of my life I've had positive feelings about my breasts, but the older I get, the more loose skin and sagginess I notice. I breastfed three babies with these two mounds of fat on my chest. So now, in my mid-forties, I'm having to reconcile my feelings about aging in relation to how my breasts look. They still look pretty nice in a bra. I will say that! *smile*

Women spend a lot of money on bras, plastic surgery, creams and potions in an effort to enhance their breasts. If you have a smaller chest, you may be worried that you don't seem as feminine as other women. But short of surgery, you're kind of stuck with what you're given. Breast size is heavily dependent on genetics. It's disheartening to me that we invest so much time and energy worrying about and obsessing over that which our genes decided for us.

And don't get me started on the industries that prey on women's lack of self-esteem when it comes to their boobs. Plastic surgeons who perform breast enhancements have made billions off those insecurities. And the folks at Victoria's Secret are rolling in dough after capitalizing on the pressure women feel to look sexy—and much of that is tied to showcasing breasts in satin and lace.

I'll be the first to admit I've bought into it—the looking sexy thing. Not so much anymore, but at one time, I bet my lingerie collection rivaled anyone's. I still have dozens of bras lying around that are beautiful but too small for me. I've finally, in my forties, learned that comfortable bras are where it's at. It helps that I don't leave the house for work and can sit here in my office in my pajamas if I want—not to mention the fact that my husband doesn't care if I wear sexy bras or not.

We'll be talking more about sex and the pressure to look and feel sexy later in the book, so let me try to get back around to boobs, alright?

The other part of the discussion—and what fuels the desire to modify our breasts from whatever their natural state might be—is the way breasts are represented and shown in all forms of media and advertising.

We see these models with impossibly perky breasts, defying the laws of gravity, and we think ours should look like that too.

First off, Photoshop and air brushing are very real things. We'll talk about that more when we discuss our "media diet," but don't believe everything you see. It's totally possible those breasts you envy have been enhanced by surgery and/or by Photoshop. What you're seeing on those models and actresses is NOT reality. It helps to remind yourself of that over and over again.

It's normal for breasts to sag. It's normal for them to be different sizes. There is much diversity when it comes to nipples and areolas, in size, shape and color. It is totally normal when you lie down for your breasts to fall toward your arms. It's normal to have loose skin and stretch marks too, especially if you've ever been pregnant or breastfed.

I know it's hard to unlink the connection we've made between breasts and femininity, but I hope through this book, you can at least get to the point of caring about them and focusing on them for YOU and not for anyone else. If you want to wear sexy bras, go for it! But don't sacrifice comfort. It's not worth it to sit around having pretty boobs if you have a wire digging into you. If you want to reserve that kind of undergarment for special occasions, dates, or boudoir photo shoots, that's certainly fine. But still, you should be wearing it because it makes YOU feel sexy or beautiful, not because there's some sort of expectation for you to look a certain way.

And I just want to speak for a moment to women who have had mastectomies or any kind of surgery that has left scars on your breasts. If you no longer have your breasts or if you have scarring, you may have a lot of negative feelings toward that part of your body. You may feel like your femininity has been lost. The letter you write in the next journaling assignment is likely to be very emotional. I don't know personally what you are going through, but I just want to tell you that you're very strong for getting through whatever caused those scars, and I know you are strong enough to love your body now in all its resilient glory.

Shall we get on with it, then? Perhaps you've received a love letter to your breasts from a lover or suitor at some point in your life. Now it's your chance to write one to the girls in your own words!

Journaling Assignment #9: Your Breasts

Write a letter to your breasts apologizing for any negative thoughts you've had about them through the years. Then list all of the positive aspects about your breasts. Finally, make a vow to focus on the positive and to do your best to love and take care of this body part, including regular screenings for lumps and other issues.

Face, Hair, and Neck, OH MY!

I decided to put these features together in one section, even though you could probably devote a letter solely to your face or hair. I threw neck in there because…well, you'll see in a moment.

Let's talk about our hair first, okay? Here's another aspect of our bodies that we probably either love or hate. Like other parts, this one also has a huge genetic component as far as color, texture, and thickness are concerned. However, unlike other body parts, this one is easy to change.

How many of you cut your hair? How about color? What about perm or straighten? Do you blow-dry it? Or curl it? There are tons of options for cuts, colors and styles, now more than ever. Just like the rest of the beauty industry preys on our insecurities, so does the hair industry, it just may seem a little more innocuous.

But how many times have you seen magazines promising hairstyles that will make you look younger, or thinner, or sexier?

All. The. Damn. Time, am I right? (You know I am.)

A great deal of our identity is tied up in our outward appearance, and our hair might be the single biggest part of that. Any time a woman seeks a makeover, what is the easiest and most striking way to transform her look? It's probably going to be changing her hair.

I'm exceedingly lucky in this area because I love my hair. It's thick; it has a naturally wavy texture; I have only a few grays (for being in my forties, so I'm not going to complain too much about that), and I have been dying it auburn for about ten years now. I have also had it blonde, as well as my natural brunette color with blonde and red highlights. But I love the auburn because it suits my personality. I chose the cover model for this book partially because of the bright colors in the photo, but the other reason was because her hair is about the same color as mine (mine's a little lighter).

But I realize not every woman has such positive feelings about their hair. The "beauty standards" say it's more feminine to have long, thick hair. Color trends change, but gray hair is usually considered to make a woman look older (though it has become trendy to have gray or silver hair as of late.) Sometimes super-straight hair is in style, and sometimes curly. Women of color may feel their natural hair isn't ideal because it doesn't conform to "beauty standards." Notice I put "beauty standards" in quotes because I think they are bullshit.

Speaking of age, we have very concrete ideas about how a woman's hair should change as she ages. There are many who feel that women over forty shouldn't have long hair (eff those people, mine currently sits several inches below my shoulders.) Women are divided about whether or not grays should be dyed away or kept natural.

No matter how you feel about your hair, you're going to have a chance to get your emotions out in our next journaling assignment, so be thinking about what you might want to say. I just want to go on record here encouraging you to have whatever hairstyle YOU feel suits YOU best. Screw all the trends and outdated notions that try to dictate our choices. If you want long fuchsia hair when you're fifty years old, GO FOR IT! If you want a short silver pixie cut at age twenty-five, GO FOR IT! The best part about playing with different hairstyles and colors is that you can change your mind. Maybe not immediately for some cuts and colors, but you can definitely try lots of different looks according to your mood and lifestyle.

Let's move on to the face and neck. I'm lumping these together since they're attached and all. I didn't want to leave out the neck because as you age, it can become a greater focus and source of insecurities than ever before. Maybe you have loose skin, or a double chin, or you have what I call ninja hairs popping up on your chin and neck. Those things are all completely normal, and maybe you want to address them in your letter in the next journaling assignment.

So now I want to talk about your face. Your face is probably the first thing people notice about you, and it's probably the part of yourself you spend the most time looking at as well. I want you to be VERY specific in your letter about your face. We have some pretty fucked-up "beauty standards" for facial features, and other than makeup and plastic surgery, you are kind of stuck with what you've got.

First off, I want to remind you what I said a little earlier in the book:

IT'S NOT YOUR JOB TO BE PRETTY.

You heard that, right? I want you to repeat that a few times before you write your letter. We are so damn critical of ourselves, even our faces, when the size and shape of our features are largely determined by factors completely beyond our control.

In your letter, I want you to think about the following:

Your eyes: "beauty standards" dictate that eyes are big and have no wrinkles around them or circles underneath, and are framed by manicured brows (thick brows are en vogue at the moment, but who knows if that will change) and long, thick lashes. Maybe your eyes are small, or you don't like the color, or you are always battling those dark circles underneath. Maybe your brows are sparse, or you have crow's feet. They say the eyes are the windows to your soul, and if you're not in love with yours, it might be a source of strife for you.

Your nose: Small, short, narrow noses have been a "beauty standard" for a while. I don't know about you, but I've never cared for my nose. I'm trying to make peace with it, though, since getting a nose job is not in my future. Maybe you think your nose is too long, too wide, your nostrils are too big. Maybe it's crooked. It seems to me—anecdotal evidence only, of course—that many women have negative opinions about their noses. Rhinoplasty sits in the top ten requested plastic surgery procedures, and one source listed it as the third most common procedure in 2017.

Your lips: Full lips with no wrinkles around them are a sign of youth. If yours are thinner or you have fine lines around them, you may feel it ages your face. I guess it's also possible to think your lips are too big/too full as well. We are so hard on ourselves!

Your cheekbones/chin: High cheekbones are a classic "beauty standard." Some women can fake it with contouring makeup, but most of us are stuck with what our Momma gave us. How do you feel about yours?

Your skin: Because we're overly obsessed with youth, women often fixate on tightening skin, filling in wrinkles, covering up age spots and freckles. I personally have a condition that causes dark patches on my otherwise fair skin. It began after my third son was born, and now every summer, it crops up on a different part of my face. It's some sort of reaction between hormones and the sun, and I'm not a big fan. However, through the body positive movement, I have come to terms with it. It doesn't make me less worthy. It's just some extra melanin.

Your teeth: You probably have lots of feelings about your teeth; I know I do. Whether they are crooked, discolored, not perfectly white, you have braces, or you're missing one or more of them, we can have a lot of anxiety about what our smiles look like, to the point where we might not even want to smile. This is another part of us we have to come to terms with and realize that no matter what condition our teeth are in, we are still worthy of happiness and love.

One final word about makeup, then I'm going to turn you loose to write your journal entry. No doubt you will have a lot to say about this very visible area of your body!

I have no problem with makeup. Some body positive activists feel like makeup is a lie, just another way to feed into those "beauty standards" I've referenced. But to me, it's kind of like the clothes you wear and how you style your hair—as long as you are doing it for YOU, I think it's totally fine. I only wear makeup if I'm going out, and it only takes me five minutes to put on. I don't feel like that's a sellout, and *I* like the way I look in it.

If you take an hour to put on your face, and you wouldn't dare let anyone see you without makeup, then you might want to reexamine your reasons for wearing it and what you're covering up with it. If it's because you're embarrassed or ashamed of the way you look without it, then I would encourage you to gradually try wearing less until you can go out in public without any at all.

I too challenge myself to go out in public without makeup on occasion. Like I've said repeatedly, and I will say one more time because it's just so damn true:

IT'S NOT MY JOB TO BE PRETTY!

Journaling Assignment #10: Face, Neck and Hair

You've probably been asking your friends and/or partner(s) what they think about your hair or face your entire life. Whether trying new makeup or a new haircut, we're always eagerly seeking other people's opinions. But right now it's time to focus on your own feelings about that part of you the entire world sees. For once, it doesn't matter if your mom doesn't like it when you wear eyeliner, or your dad is mad because you cut your hair off. It's all about what YOU think.

Write a letter to your face, neck, and hair and apologize for the times you've dissed them in the past. Then list some reasons you actually like them, like maybe your eyes are a pretty color, or you have nice lashes, or maybe you like your ears. Finally, promise them that in the future you're going to focus on the positive parts—and remember that a lot of things about your face are things you can't change. (This is also where you can blame your mom or maybe your grandma for giving you sparse eyebrows or a long nose!)

THE FAT GIRL'S GUIDE TO LOVING YOUR BODY

Hey, you know something I forgot? Body Hair

I'm not going to make you write a letter to your body hair (though if the spirit moves you, don't let me stand in your way!) but I did want to discuss it briefly. Body hair removal is a multi-billion-dollar industry. Maybe not as huge as the weight loss industry, but those Venus razor people are making a killing (have you seen how much those blades cost?) There've also been a whole slew of new products on the market, not to mention more sophisticated (and pricier) options like laser hair removal. All of it is focused on getting rid of something that is completely 100% natural.

I never thought much about why women are taught to shave certain parts of their body until about ten years ago when I was getting divorced and wading back into the dating pool (huh, sounds like the premise of my book *Fat Girl*, only I assure you, my ex is NOTHING like Jeremy, thank god!) In any case, I joined a site called OKCupid. Ever heard of it? Well, as dating sites go, I actually think it's one of the better ones, but I digress.

In any case, they have a feature on this site, or at least they used to (I haven't been on it in ages) where you respond to a series of questions. One of them states something like this:

Women are obligated to shave their legs.

So you are supposed to choose whether you agree or disagree with the statement. I once wrote a huge rant about this question in some blog post, I think. In any case, I just couldn't get over the word "obligated."

If anyone truly thinks women are *obligated* to shave their legs, I'd really like to smack said person upside the head.

That would be like insisting men are obligated to shave their balls. Can you really see men across the planet taking razors, lasers and Nair to their balls because they want to please their partners? I mean, yes, some men already do this. But can you imagine it at the same level as women who actually *do* feel *obligated* to shave for their partners? And not just their coochies but their LEGS! We're talking some major real estate here. And, of course, we're expected to shave our armpits as well.

Then there's the whole facial hair removal industry for women. Not just eyebrow maintenance, but upper lip waxing, chin hair removal, all that fun stuff.

How much time and money do you spend removing hair from your body—hair that is perfectly 100% natural?

I'm not saying you should stop shaving or whatever your hair removal method of choice is.

All I'm saying is that you might want to re-examine your routine or at least your reasons for doing it. If you ever feel bad, guilty, ashamed, less attractive, less feminine, etc. because of your body hair, PLEASE remember that humans are mammals, and mammals have body hair. That's just the way we're made, okay? You can thank millions of years of evolution, if that's your jam. Or you can thank God or whatever higher power you believe in. One way or another: YOU WERE CREATED WITH BODY HAIR.

And that's all I've got to say about that.

Saving the Best for Last: Your Insides

It shouldn't come as a surprise that I firmly believe the very best, most remarkable, and special parts of you are the parts on the inside. Your body is merely a shell that holds your brain, your heart, and your soul. I could probably write a book about each one of those parts, but we're here to talk about your body, right? It's true, but so much of what goes on in our heads and hearts impacts our bodies and how we feel about our bodies.

Your brain is the most powerful tool you have for fighting self-shaming and self-loathing. There have been millions (probably, I mean, I haven't actually counted them) studies about how important psychology and self-talk are to our well-being. How we think about ourselves and talk about ourselves has, I think, the greatest impact on how we view our bodies.

And, this entire book, if it could be distilled into just one simple statement, would give us something like: *training our brains to love and accept our bodies*.

But beyond how you feel about your body, your brain is where a lot of other amazing shit goes down. It's responsible for problem-solving, forming speech, and making sense of the world around us. We can even use it to do truly monumental tasks like calculus or rocket science (pretty sure there's some overlap there.) We can memorize The Gettysburg Address and store memories of what happened at our sixth birthday parties. We can use our brains to create art, whether that art involves words, music, or paints and canvases. The brain is a pretty incredible organ—I would argue the MOST incredible organ, so in a moment when I ask you to write a letter to your insides, I want you to feel free to brag about your brain like the proud mom of a kid who just made straight As on her report card.

So what does your heart have to do with this? Isn't the whole "heart" ideal overplayed from a scientific point of view? After all, your heart's job is to pump blood; you don't actually manufacture feelings in your heart. That stuff goes down in your brain too!

Well, of course, it does. But for the purposes of this book, we're looking at our hearts as the center of our emotions, the metaphorical place where we harbor both positive and negative feelings about people, places, and ideas. We often illustrate the dichotomy of thinking versus feeling with using your head versus using your heart, so that's what we're going to do here as well.

Your heart is probably a beautiful place. Think about the capacity you have for love. How many people on this earth do you truly love? Maybe you include your parents, your partner, or your progeny—maybe pets as well. I'm guessing you could quickly make a list of all the people and animals you love unconditionally. It's not your thighs that make that possible, or your elbows or armpits, or even your pinky toes. It's your heart. Your heart is infinitely more important, valuable, and noteworthy than your belly, isn't it?

And I also want to take a moment to appeal to you on a spiritual level. It doesn't matter what religion you subscribe to, if you believe you have a soul inside you, then please listen up to this next little bit. Maybe you believe your soul is designated for a heavenly purpose. Maybe you feel your soul's purpose is to change the world or discover the cure for cancer. It doesn't matter what you believe, it's the idea that there is something beyond your corporal body that will live on after you are gone, your legacy, if you will. Whether you believe in an actual afterlife, or only that you will leave behind memories—ask yourself what YOU want to be known for, what kind of legacy you're creating for those you leave behind.

If you're miserable with your body and in your life, that doesn't seem like how you'd want others to remember you. It doesn't sound like the purpose a soul would be created for, no matter how you believe you were created.

I grew up with evangelical Christian beliefs (might be hard for some of my readers to believe considering the topics of some of my racier romances, but it's true). I still retain most of those beliefs (but not in a judgy, *you're going to hell if you don't believe what I believe* kind of way), and I believe God put me on earth to do many things, but one of them was to do this, to be a role model for body positivity. I also believe God made my body, and He wouldn't want me to hate it, because I was made in His image. And you can do the math on that, right? So, if you have Christian beliefs, then put that in your pipe and smoke it.

But not literally, 'cause smoking's bad for you, m'kay?

Journaling Assignment #11: It's What's on the Inside That Counts

Write a letter to your brain, heart, and soul listing all the wonderful things about them. Then promise your insides that you'll do better to control your thoughts and feelings when it comes to disparaging your body.

Now Let's Put it All Together

So this is where I am going to be extremely hypocritical and confusing. I just spent the last part of the book asking you to break down your body into individual parts to analyze, examine, and even write letters to. It felt weird, right? And you probably are wondering if you can send me your therapy bills. But there's a method to my madness (well, there's definitely madness, anyway!)

Now that you've looked at your body from the bottom to the top and thought about your feet, legs, butt, hips, waist, belly, arms, back, shoulders, face, neck, hair and insides, I want you to STOP thinking of your body as all those individual parts.

Too often we are consumed with anxiety about one or two body parts. We form unhealthy obsessions with our thighs or our bellies. We can't see the forest for the trees, so to speak.

It's cliché AF, but it still rings true:

You are greater than the sum of your parts.

When you add up all the parts I listed, it may sound like an anatomy lesson, not a living, breathing human being, which is what you are. Your value is in the unique combination of all of those parts, especially the inside ones we just discussed. Try to think of your body as a whole (including the inside parts) when you look at it or think about it, and when you talk about it to others.

Dealing with Body- and Fat-Shamers 101

If you are a person of size, you have probably at some point in your life been bullied or treated differently because of your size. Sometimes people are rude and obnoxious right to your face. Other times, you're the victim of the type of micro-aggressions I mentioned earlier in the book. Sometimes, poor treatment is extremely subtle.

As someone who has been everything from a size 8 to a size 22 at my current height, I have seen firsthand how differently I am treated when I'm thinner versus fatter. There is a certain point on the scale where I'm nearly invisible if I'm over it. It's baffling! How can someone taking up so much space not be noticed? But it's totally true. I wouldn't be surprised if some of you can relate.

There are fat-haters out there who don't believe fat people should be seen. Or that we deserve to be happy. Or that we deserve to find love. And what I can't understand is exactly how are we hurting them?

We already talked about all of the stereotypes and falsehoods perpetuated about fat people. These fat-haters are the ones responsible for keeping those stereotypes alive. They have a few stock insults and so-called "well-intentioned" responses I'm going to now go over so you know how to respond if you're struck by one of these dung-nuggets!

Hey, Were You Aware You're Fat?

One of the more asinine pieces of feedback fat people get both in person and on social media is just the simple statement that we are indeed fat—in case we didn't know, apparently. Well-meaning folks feel it is their duty to point it out to us on the off chance we are unaware we have bigger bodies.

It's exceedingly difficult for me to come up with a response to this kind of statement that is anything other than pure, unadulterated snark.

-*Oh, wow, thanks for pointing that out. I actually had no clue I was fat.*

-*Oh, really? Well, were you aware that you have a nose and two ears?*

-*Gosh, what would fat people do if we didn't have straight-sized strangers constantly reminding us that we're bigger than they are?!*

-*Thanks, Captain Obvious!*

Feel free to come up with your own responses.

The other insinuation when you hear some idiot telling you you're fat is that you don't know about dieting or weight loss programs and products. Apparently you've been living under some rock for the past several decades, and Weight Watchers, Atkins, South Beach, Keto, Jenny Craig, Nutrisystem, etc. are all foreign concepts to you.

What Captain Obvious and his ilk don't seem to realize is that fat folks are not only familiar with every single diet known to mankind, but we've also tried them. We know so much about nutrition, we could probably become professional nutritionists. We aren't fat because of a lack of knowledge. There are a million reasons that someone might be fat, but I can almost guarantee you that every fat person has tried at least one diet in their lifetime. And I'd be willing to bet that most of us have tried them all.

But You're Glorifying Obesity!

If you follow Tess Holliday, the plus-sized model, on social media, you'll see this peppered in the comments on her posts: "You're glorifying obesity."

Let's break that down a bit, shall we? What exactly do the haters mean by "glorifying?" Well, glorifying something means you are revering it, promoting it. Basically it means making obesity out to be so awesome that all the cool kids want to do it. I don't exactly see a lot of folks working hard to become fat, which they would be if obesity was actually being "glorified." Fat people are regularly marginalized and stigmatized, so I don't see people rushing out to voluntarily bring that upon themselves.

I fail to see how a woman posting a photo of herself on social media is promoting obesity. I could share a photo of myself eating dinner, but it doesn't mean I'm promoting whatever food I'm eating. I post photos of my dog a lot on Instagram (heck, she even has her own account), but that doesn't mean I'm promoting dog ownership. It just means I have a damn cute puppy, and I want to share her cuteness with other dog lovers.

I hate to break it to you, but fat people exist. They actually lead normal lives, and sometimes, in the course of those lives, they like to post photos of themselves on social media, just like other straight-sized folks do. What a crazy notion! Fat people doing normal stuff is not glorifying obesity. It's just them existing and living their lives.

Oh, but what if it's a *model* like Tess or Ashley Graham or whatever other plus-sized models you can think of. So it's glorifying obesity if we see fat women wear fashionable clothes or *gulp* look sexy, even? Because fat people aren't allowed to look fashionable or look sexy—or be sexy, or feel sexy, or have anything to do with sex, apparently. See above where fat people have just as much right to carry on normal lives as anyone else—and that includes being interested in and having sex.

Obviously, anyone who says photos or videos of fat people glorify obesity is just a giant tool, and if someone tells you you're doing that, feel free to call them out on it.

But You Have Such a Pretty Face

It's truly hard to think of a more backhanded compliment than this. I have heard this one a time or two myself—though not lately. Maybe my face isn't pretty anymore, I don't know. Nor do I care! In any case, you know what I'm going to say, right? I've said it so many times already in this book you're probably going to hear it in your sleep:

IT'S NOT YOUR JOB TO BE PRETTY.

Likewise, it's not your job to be thin. Pretty and fat are not mutually exclusive. The backhandedness here is that "Oh, your face is pretty, but the rest of you, not so much. You need to lose weight so your body will match the attractiveness level of your face."

If you've actually said this to someone, shame on you. Maybe you didn't realize what a horrible thing it is to say, but it is, just in case you were wondering.

If someone says this to you, honestly, I'd probably tell them to fuck off. But, hey, that's me. But maybe you could say something a little less brash instead. Perhaps smile sweetly and say, "I *do* have a pretty face, thank you for noticing. And the rest of me is pretty amazing too."

If not, then the fuck off thing is perfectly appropriate as far as I'm concerned.

I Wish I Had Your Confidence

This backhanded compliment is the cousin of "But you have such a pretty face." This is one I still hear. A LOT. Especially on my Phoebe Alexander Instagram, where I've been known to show myself half-naked. I also hear, "You're so brave!"

People who say this, and it's almost always women, think they are admitting to being a little envious of you, which in turn will validate you.

But nope. Let me tell you what I hear when people say, "I wish I had your confidence."

I hear: *I'm not even half as big as you are, and there's no way in hell I could post pictures of myself in a bikini. You're so brave for putting yourself out there like that when you look like you do.*

If you hear something like this, trust me when I say it reflects much more on the self-esteem of the person saying it than it does on you.

I tell people it has nothing to do with confidence or bravery. It has to do with refusing to let society dictate what I wear and how I behave. If you do have someone say this to you, it may feel like an insult, but try to take it to mean you're way farther along in your bopo journey than they are. Hopefully you can be a good role model for them.

But I'm Concerned About Your Health!

This is a super common statement you hear from fat- and body-shamers. Just look at the comments on any post or article about fat people online, and there will be an army of supposedly well-meaning folks claiming the reason they hate fat people is because they are concerned about their health.

In the entire history of bullshit, I'm not sure there's ever been any deeper, nastier or more vile than this statement.

First off, there is no way to tell if someone is healthy by looking at them.

There are very healthy fat people (I am one of them).

There are very unhealthy skinny people.

And everything in between.

A few responses to this particular statement come to mind. First off, my health—and your health, too, for that matter—is none of their business. Are they a doctor? No? Then maybe he or she should worry about whatever job they actually get paid to do.

My health is actually pretty fan-fucking-tastic. Every time I do go to the doctor (which isn't very often—see my chapter about dealing with medical professionals), they seem personally affronted that they can't find anything wrong with me. My blood pressure is good. My blood sugar is usually below normal. My cholesterol level is fine. I don't take any medications besides ibuprofen. The only chronic medical issues I have are completely unrelated to my weight: migraines and really horrific periods (I'm going to talk about that later too! Oh joy!)

But you know what? It doesn't matter if you're healthy or not. Not only is it extremely invasive and, frankly, creepy for some stranger to tell you they're worried about your health, but even if you have health issues, are you not allowed to exist? Are you not allowed to have a life? To enjoy yourself? To feel good about yourself? OF COURSE YOU ARE!

Furthermore, does this health-concerned person troll social media posts written by drinkers and smokers, imploring them to change their ways because of health concerns? I highly doubt it. What about cancer patients? Or muscular sclerosis or lupus or allergies? They aren't seeking these folks out on the internet to tell them they're concerned about their health?

If people are really concerned about health, maybe they should try to change our healthcare system so that it is affordable, so that everyone has coverage, and so that preventative treatments are covered—instead of it being a for-profit system where the CEOs of health insurance companies are billionaires. Maybe they should worry about why junk food and highly processed foods are cheaper than whole foods, and why the latter is not as accessible to those in low-income areas. Or maybe they should worry about the opioid epidemic—and, guess what, being addicted to opioids is way more dangerous and unhealthy than being fat.

Oh, they aren't doing any of that stuff…so that must mean they're just fatphobic assholes, after all. That's what I thought.

Sometimes people who use this fat-shaming "reasoning" think that by being extra combative and "shamey" that they can influence fat people to "take control of their health and lose weight." But all the evidence actually points to the opposite happening. The more people are shamed about their bodies or weight, the heavier they become. You can read more about it here:

https://labblog.uofmhealth.org/body-work/fat-shaming-wont-solve-obesity-science-might

https://www.washingtonpost.com/news/to-your-health/wp/2014/09/11/fat-shaming-doesnt-work-a-new-study-says/

https://www.theatlantic.com/health/archive/2015/12/fat-shaming-on-the-london-underground/418110/

https://www.healthline.com/nutrition/fat-shaming-makes-things-worse#obesity-risk

Feel free to share those articles with any of the fat-shamers in your life. But guess what—you also get to write them a letter! Stay tuned for your next journaling assignment.

Journaling Assignment #12: A Letter to Body- and Fat-Shamers

In what ways have you been body- or fat-shamed in your life? Think back on one instance (I know most of us can think of many) and write a letter to your shamer telling them how their comment affected you. Feel free to make it nice and constructive, if you'd like. Or if you're angry AF, feel free to write a rage-filled diatribe. This is for YOU, after all. Only you know which method is going to be most cathartic for you.

You have had people in your life—people who know and supposedly love you, as well as perfect strangers—comment on your body in a way that is unfair and completely inappropriate. Your body is no one else's business but your own, and if people have made the comments I just outlined to you, then they were wrong. This is your chance to tell them.

Dealing with the Medical Community

Did you like that segue way? I went from the "concerned about your health" to actual medical/health stuff. Nailed it!

Most of what I'm going to say in this chapter is strictly my opinion and informed by forty-some years of dealing with doctors myself, but if you go searching for evidence to back up my points, you're likely to find it.

Fatphobia runs rampant among the medical community. There's a meme floating around with a fat lady whose arm is falling off and bleeding profusely. The doctor looks at her and says, "All you need to do is lose some weight!"

I can't tell you how many times I've been fat- or body-shamed in my life by doctors and nurses. There's usually a sense of shock when they go to take my blood pressure and it's perfect. Or when they order glucose tests because, surely at this weight I'm diabetic, and they come back completely normal. But, boy, were they hoping to pin whatever ailment brought me into their office on something obesity-related.

Doctors are very good at establishing a picture in their minds of what is normal. They run tests that produce a result within a certain range, and anyone not within those limits or parameters is "abnormal." For being reasonably intelligent individuals, and arguably among the most highly educated of all of us, it's ludicrous they can't grasp the concept that "normal" is not the same for everyone.

There was a point when this became abundantly clear to me. When I had my second miscarriage in a row back in 1999, I did loads and loads of research about what the issue might be. Everything seemed to point to luteal phase defect, which involves a lack of progesterone to support a growing embryo. I took my findings to my doctor, and he ordered a progesterone test. I already knew from my research that many doctors didn't believe luteal phase defect was a thing because some women could carry a baby to term with very low progesterone.

My test results came back with a level somewhere between seven and eight. Everything I'd read pointed to levels needing to be at least fifteen. Apparently, that was an updated level over what my gynecologist had been taught. He said eight should be fine. I brought up a crazy idea he seemed to be blown away by:

What if I personally need a higher level to maintain a pregnancy?

Sure, some women are able to maintain pregnancies with levels lower than eight, but what if *I* needed a fifteen or a twenty to carry a baby?

So he agreed to a luteal phase defect treatment regimen, and guess what? My son Jordan was born in 2000, after a course of Clomid and progesterone suppositories. I did the same routine with my third son, who was born in 2005.

That leads me to the point of what is right for your body may not work for someone else's body and vice versa. Doctors want to treat everyone the same, but the truth is that we're all different and have unique body chemistry. I understand that doctors need to know baselines and have standards of care—but they also need to be flexible and keep in mind an individual's unique needs.

The other problem is that the medical community changes their minds about stuff all the time. Remember back in the 80s when fat was the worst thing ever? They cut the fat out of all kinds of foods and instead put a bunch of chemicals in. Now the medical community has finally realized that all those chemicals are bad news. Imagine that!

Neither one of those points has to do with fatphobia, but they do combine with fatphobia to result in fat people receiving inferior care compared to their thinner counterparts. This results in

- Misdiagnoses
- Late diagnoses
- Poorer patient outcomes
- Fat patients being less likely to seek medical care

Some studies have shown that doctors treat fat patients' pain differently than thinner patients', often prescribing smaller doses of pain medication or no medications at all. Some doctors minimize fat people's pain or feel they *deserve* the pain they're in because their bodies are larger.

Doctors frequently encourage weight loss during visits that have nothing to do with weight. The arm falling off meme I shared above is an extreme example, but how many times have fat people been told to lose weight when they have the flu, allergies, or endometriosis?

Plus, let's not forget there are many medical conditions that can lead to weight gain. Polycystic Ovarian Syndrome comes to mind, as well as hypothyroidism, Cushing's syndrome, and depression. Certain medications can cause weight gain as well. If you have any of these conditions or take medications that lead to weight gain, you'll probably spend a lot of time in doctors' offices, and I bet you have some horrifying stories you could contribute to this chapter.

Avoiding the doctor is really not an option. Sometimes we really do need doctors' expertise to get or stay healthy. They have access to testing and equipment, not to mention medications, that can be the difference between life and death. In no way am I advocating avoiding seeing a doctor for both well and sick visits. It's an area I'm still working on, and I really do want to practice what I preach. I haven't been to see a doctor in about two years now. Granted, I haven't had health issues, either. But I have gotten so fed up with the poor care I've received in my life that I haven't been particularly motivated to undergo a well visit. I am making a resolution to change that in 2020, though!

There are some things you can do to ensure you get better care. Here are some ideas:

- First off: remember that you deserve to be treated with respect, and you have a fundamental right to address your health concerns, the same as any person.

- If you do experience weight bias, the Obesity Action Coalition invites you to fill out the Weight Bias Reporting Form: https://www.obesityaction.org/action-center/report-weight-bias-issues/

- Check out the Health at Every Size website where you can search for professionals who treat people of all sizes with respect: https://haescommunity.com/search/

- If you do come across a fatphobic doctor, remember there are other doctors in the world (and even in your town!) You don't have to see a doctor who doesn't respect you as a person. Walk away and find someone else. It may take longer to get the care you need, but it will be better, trust me. There are many times in my life when I SHOULD have done this but didn't. And now here I am having lost respect in the medical community as a whole—which is just as judgy and biased as fatphobic doctors. I know they aren't all like that!

- If you're uncomfortable being weighed, or if you're recovering from an eating disorder, simply tell the nurse or doctor you'd prefer not to be weighed. Often, doctors can treat you without knowing the number on the scale. Alternatively, ask that you be allowed to turn around or close your eyes while they record the number without comment. If your doctor is truly a compassionate person—you wouldn't want to be treated by anyone who wasn't, right?—she will find a way to make you comfortable.

- Take a loved one or friend with you for support. Bonus points if they have a big mouth and will call out disrespectful behavior if it crops up!

- Self-care is of the utmost importance. If anxiety kicks in, feel free to reschedule your appointment if your symptoms aren't urgent.

- Try to go in with the attitude that the doctor likely has good intentions. Don't go in expecting to be treated poorly. That's not fair to the doctor, who hopefully means well and isn't sizeist.

- If you have a chronic illness or you need to seek medical treatment often, and it triggers anxiety for you, consider seeing a therapist as well. She should be able to help you develop coping strategies for undergoing medical treatment.

So what if you *do* want to lose weight?

There could be many reasons we want to change our bodies—and they don't all have to be imprudent. Maybe you have a health issue, and your doctor feels weight loss will help (a legitimate reason, unlike some of the examples I gave in the previous section). Or perhaps you want to relieve stress on joints or improve your mobility. I hope after reading this book, you'll choose to make your goal unrelated to weight. For example, your goal could be to be able to walk farther or lift heavier weights. Or perhaps it's to bring down your AC1 level or cholesterol. No matter what goal you choose, it should be for YOU and not for your partner or to meet societal expectations.

This is an area I've honestly struggled with a great deal since finding body positivity. And maybe since I don't have it all figured out, I'm not the best person to speak on it, but I still think it's worth a shot because it's a very real issue. I'm sure I'm not the only one struggling to reconcile wanting to love my body while also wanting to be fitter.

One of the things I've had to do is closely examine my motives for wanting to lose weight. I've lost large quantities of weight many times in my forty-some-odd years, and it's almost never been for the right reasons. When I was a teenager, I wanted to be more accepted. I wanted to gain male attention; I'm not even going to lie about that. When I was a young mother, I didn't want people to think I'd "let my body go" just because I'd popped out a couple of kids. When I was in my early and mid-thirties, it was because I wanted to be able to wear certain clothes. It was very much a pride and vanity sort of thing each time.

I will fully admit that in the past, my motives for losing weight were never health-related or for ME. The reasons I just listed aren't good reasons for changing your body. Maybe that's why I was only successful up to a point, and then I'd gain the weight back (plus additional pounds).

When I suffered from an eating disorder, and I now realize I was suffering up until the time I discovered body positivity, I was completely obsessive about losing weight. I counted every calorie and journaled it either in a notebook or in a spreadsheet on my computer (oh yeah, I'm a total data nerd, so charting weight loss filled a sick, twisted need). I also tracked my weight and body measurements with all the dedication and preciseness of NASA engineers tracking a rocket on its way into outer space.

Imagine how I felt when I accidentally let myself binge, when I lost control. Imagine how I felt when the scale picked up a couple of pounds because I'd eaten too much salt, or I had PMS.

I felt like a complete failure. And you probably don't have to *imagine*—you've probably had those exact same feelings yourself.

If I legitimately wanted to get into better shape after I discovered body positivity, certain conditions would need to be met:

- I wouldn't be able to count calories or track my weight. It couldn't be about weight at all.
- Measuring tapes and scales would be off-limits.
- I'd have to find a different way of measuring my progress.

I can't tell you what will work for *you*, but I *will* tell you what's worked for me in the past six months or so. I know it worked because I have more energy, can walk farther, and my clothes are looser. When I'm taking care of myself like this, my back also feels a LOT better.

I made it all about moving and listening to my body. More specifically:

- Like I mentioned before, I practice intuitive eating, eating what my body tells me to eat and when my body tells me to eat. That means most of my meals happen between 10 AM and 6 PM because that's what naturally feels right to me.
- By not making any foods off-limits, I am way much likely to binge eat.
- I focus on trying to eat more whole foods. I haven't been doing too well with this in the past month or two, but I plan to get back to it. I really do feel better when I'm eating foods with higher nutritional value. Notice I did not say GOOD foods!
- But the most important thing I did was add more exercise into my day. In June, I began walking twice a day. The one thing I allow myself to track is steps! I still have a hard time reaching 10,000 per day (which is the recommended amount) because I have such a sedentary job, but I usually can get to 7-8,000 with no problem. In October, my husband and I adopted a rescue puppy to help in this endeavor, among other reasons. When winter comes, I won't be able to stay inside where it's warm and toasty. The puppy (she is adorable, by the way, and has her own Instagram account here: www.instagram.com/indy.the.shepsky) will have to be taken out to walk no matter what the weather is. She has a LOT of energy too!
- The one thing I haven't added back to the routine yet but plan to is strength training. Pump some iron! It's so good for you, and it really boosts your metabolism too.

The main idea is to make the focus on taking care of yourself and not on losing weight. And there are plenty of ways to measure your progress besides stepping on a scale. Some weight-loss programs call these Non-Scale Victories (or NSVs for short). Though I don't recommend any weight-loss programs, I don't have any problem with the term NSV, so here are some to consider:

- Do you have more energy?
- Are you able to walk farther?
- Are you becoming more flexible?
- Are you becoming stronger? Can you lift more weight and do more reps?
- Has your sleep improved?
- Has your digestion improved?
- Do you notice a difference in your mood?
- Are everyday tasks getting easier?
- Do you seem to get sick less often?
- Does your mind feel sharper and clearer?
- If you've had bloodwork done, have the numbers improved?
- Are you taking less medication?
- Has your relationship with food improved?
- Have you enjoyed being out in nature more because of your increased stamina and fitness?

Journaling Assignment #13: All the Diets

I'd like you to spend a few moments thinking about all the diets you've tried in your life. What are some of them? How did they make you feel? Were any of them sustainable? Reflect on why dieting isn't the answer. Need some inspiration? Feel free to read these articles first:

bit.ly/FGGLink4

bit.ly/FGGLink5

bit.ly/FGGLink6

bit.ly/FGGLink7y

THE FAT GIRL'S GUIDE TO LOVING YOUR BODY

More on Exercise

A lot of fat people have a love/hate relationship with exercise. And is it any wonder? We're vilified for not working out, called couch potatoes and all kinds of nasty names. Yet if we are seen in public working out, we're often ridiculed. It. Makes. No. Sense. Right?

Let me make one thing clear from the get-go: I am *not* athletic. I am probably the least athletic person you will ever meet because I lack any coordination whatsoever. I can't throw a football, shoot a basketball, kick a soccer ball, play tennis or anything else that requires hand-eye-foot coordination. The ONE semi-athletic thing I can do is swim. Though, I am always reminded of what George Carlin said about swimming. He basically said it's not a sport; it's a way to keep from drowning.

However, I grew up in a family where exercise was revered, especially by my father. Now, my father was athletic (at 75, he's probably still more athletic than I could ever dream of being), and do you want to know where I got my obsession with data and tracking from? Oh, yeah, it was definitely from my dad. From the time I was born (or even before, I don't know for sure), he tracked all of his physical activity with an elaborate points system that he kept in file folders in his home office. He could tell you how many miles he's run or how many hours he's played basketball.

Despite the fact that some of my body image issues came from my parents, the importance they placed upon exercise and physical activity was a very positive influence in my life. I grew up walking, running, and swimming. We played kickball and softball in the backyard. My brother and sister and I played every form of tag known to mankind, and I had a neighborhood I could ride my bike around (and it was back in the eighties, so kids could run around all day without parents freaking out.)

There is one simple fact that I cannot deny: I feel better when I'm physically active.

Physical activity wards off depression (which I suffer from). It helps with mobility. If I start having achy joints or my back starts to hurt, it's probably because I haven't been active enough. It helps me sleep better, and it helps stabilize my moods. There is literally *nothing* negative about exercise in my book (both literally and figuratively!)

And guess what! Exercise doesn't need to have anything to do with weight loss. You can move your body simply because that's what it was designed to do. And you can move it in all sorts of ways: yoga, walking, swimming, hiking, tennis, dancing. There are so many physical activities to choose from, I would have a hard time believing you can't find one or two you actually enjoy.

That's really the key: find activities you personally enjoy. If you hate running, then don't do it. If you hate walking, well, that sucks, but you can probably find other ways to move your body. The point is to move your body; it doesn't even matter how.

I also have to put in another plug for strength training, also known as weightlifting. Even though I haven't been very consistent about doing this as of late, I know from past experience how much better I feel when I'm regularly lifting weights. You can pick up some five- or ten-pound dumbbells pretty cheaply, or there are also resistance bands you can use. Heck, in a pinch you could get a gallon of milk or a brick or landscaping stone from your yard. Or lift a kid if you've got one of those handy. Weightlifting makes a huge difference in my metabolism and overall well-being.

I mentioned in the last section about how, when I was suffering from my eating disorder, I tended to get carried away with tracking my weight, calories and measurements. I don't do any of that anymore, but tracking my steps is one thing I do allow myself to do. I haven't (as of yet) found any harm in it, and I don't get so obsessive that I go out late at night to get the rest of my steps in. I do have a friend who confesses to doing that—and more power to her. I mean, if you're going to obsess over something, I can think of a lot worse things than how many steps you walk. I wear a FitBit, and I use it mainly to track steps and sleep. Most days I get about 7000-8000 steps. I have a hard time getting to the recommended 10K because I spend so much time on my ass in my office working. I work about twelve to fourteen hours a day. I know, I know, it's an excuse. But I have a puppy now, and she really does help me get more steps in. When she's a little older and can walk farther, I'm going to be putting a lot of miles on this FitBit of mine, I can tell you that.

If you're going to exercise, definitely invest in the right kind of footwear and clothing for whatever you choose to do. I learned the hard way how big of a difference the right shoes make. I had worn the same athletic shoes for probably two or three years by the time I started walking regularly last spring. I was only a few weeks in when I realized my right heel hurt all the time, especially when I got out of bed in the morning. I didn't think much of it until July when I was preparing for a visit from my parents. I was spending almost every day on my feet painting and trying to wrangle my house into some sort of order (it was not an easy feat, let me tell you.) At that point, I was in so much pain that I could barely walk when I first got out of bed.

That was when I realized I had plantar fasciitis in my right foot. I still didn't connect it to my footwear until I tried all the regular remedies like the splint you sleep in, the support socks, and the weird ball thing you run your foot over. It was in August that I decided to buy new shoes. I researched which shoes were best for plantar fasciitis, and holy cow did that make all the difference in the world. Sometimes I still have a flare-up if I wear other shoes too much (like right now, I am wearing the hell out of my tall boots), but I wonder if I'd just gotten new shoes when I first started having pain back in the spring if I could have avoided the full-on horribleness I dealt with all summer.

Same thing goes for wearing sports bras and spandex and all that fun and happy stuff. Just use the right tools for the job, okay?

And if you haven't ever exercised, or it's been a long time, you might want to consult a medical professional before doing too much. I think I have to tell you that so you don't run off and sue me if you break a leg skiing or something (*"But Krista told me to be more active!"*) And if you *do* decide to visit a doctor, make sure to read my chapter on dealing with the medical community first.

Female Stuff

I intended this book for women, so I'm not going to shy away from talking about periods and lady bits. If a man happens to be reading (I wouldn't discourage a man from reading; after all, bopo is for everyone), then maybe you should skip this chapter? Or not, maybe you will learn something. *shrugs* I will also say this section is geared toward cis women. I can't even begin to speak on the type of hormonal issues a trans woman or trans man might have, nor can I delve into the specialized issues they face when it comes to body image. I can only imagine how difficult that journey must be, and I don't feel at all qualified to speak on it. However, I hope some of what I share might resonate with you, even if you're not a cis woman. If you're taking female hormones, you definitely know some of what I'm talking about!

I am in my forties, and I got my first period when I was ten, so I've been having periods for over thirty years. And you know what? They STILL suck. Some of you may be in menopause, and that comes with its own lovely issues. I'm not there yet, but I do have that to look forward to in the next decade or so.

But basically the reason I wanted to include this chapter is because I would be neglecting a huge part of body positivity if I didn't talk about our uteruses, vaginas, vulvas, estrogen and progesterone—basically all the female stuff. I don't know about you, but many of the changes I've seen in my body throughout the years have been in direct relation to hormones and/or being a woman.

First, and maybe this happened to you as well, I gained a lot of weight in the couple of years leading up to and the first couple of years after my period started. I was a chubby kid, and I was bullied and ridiculed a lot for it. It's funny now to look back (not *haha* funny, but *sad* funny—you know what I mean?) because I wasn't really that big, but it was back in the mid-eighties when we were starting to get obsessive about fitness and being toned and all that. By today's standards, maybe no one would have even thought I was big for my age. Well, in any case, it had a profound impact on me, as you might imagine.

I reached puberty early, yet I was the youngest kid in my class. Not a good combination, but I can only imagine how much worse it would have been if my parents and the school would have delayed me starting kindergarten for an extra year. *Oy.* I don't even want to go there.

Here I'd been this happy kid with all these interests, and all the sudden I had this very unwanted menstrual cycle and all the accoutrements (cramps, stomach upset, headaches, etc.) I know that was when my hatred of my body really started. I wish I could go back and tell that little girl that it would be okay, and things would get better, and to enjoy the last few years of childhood. I feel like they were stolen from me, in a way, because I looked a lot like I was in high school even when I was only eleven or twelve years old. I was once out shopping with my dad and was mistaken for his wife, if that tells you anything. It was positively horrifying to me as a pre-teen.

The next time my body changed a lot was when I got pregnant. I was twenty-two, and I'd just graduated from college. I'd just lost about fifty pounds during my senior year of college by starving myself and over-exercising. You can imagine how devastated I was when I gained every single one of those pounds back plus around thirty more when I was pregnant with my first son.

Let me tell you, hormones wreak havoc on me. I'm one of those ladies who gets vicious PMS, and I swear it gets worse as I age. I was the teenage girl who had to go to the nurse's office and beg to go home because I had cramps. And they were legit too, because my mom was a teacher so I couldn't call her to pick me up—I had to call my father. Any teen girl who is willing to tell her dad she needs to go home because she has cramps is not making that shit up.

So the whole reason I'm including this section is to talk about how our very identities as women, and the very things that make us so shape our feelings toward our bodies. Our bodies undergo changes every month and with pregnancy that men never experience. So I think it would be a mistake to dismiss or ignore this topic, don't you?

First off, hormonal shifts, whether they're due to pregnancy, periods, or menopause, are wild. Estrogen and progesterone are some freakin' powerful chemicals. I don't know about you, but when my hormones are in flux, I often feel out of control, depressed, helpless, anxious, hopeless, or some combination thereof. Do those feelings affect how I see my body? Hell yes they do. Do they affect how I take care of myself? Oh, yeah. Big time.

I am much more likely to consume vast quantities of sugar and fat when I am PMSing, how about you? And I am much less likely to get enough sleep and exercise. That combination often leads to me feeling like poop on a platter.

One of the things I've tried to do since I discovered body positivity is to be kinder to myself when those hormonal fluctuations are in progress. I try to be deliberate and recognize what is going on inside me. I can't stop it from happening, but I can be more patient with myself and try to cut myself some slack.

It's also important to note there's a point where PMS crosses the line into PMDD (pre-menstrual dysphoric disorder.) And there is a point where "baby blues" crosses the line into PPD (post-partum depression). If you suspect you're having a hard time carrying on with your normal life routines (work, relationships, etc.) and suspect hormones are to blame, please don't hesitate to reach out to a doctor or mental health professional.

Here are a few articles on the topic:

Bit.ly/FGGLink8

Bit.ly/FGGLink9

Bit.ly/FGGLink10

Bit.ly/FGGLink11

The other thing I wanted to talk about with regard to female stuff is female anatomy, particularly external anatomy. I didn't realize until a few years ago that some women had been conditioned to be very anxious and embarrassed about their labia and vulvas. I guess it's because of porn being so accessible. Did you know that some plastic surgeons perform labiaplasties, where they go in and surgically alter the size or shape of the labia? There is a whole industry devoted to what's called "vaginal rejuvenation," too. If you've had a baby vaginally, you may have even felt like you needed some rejuvenation down there.

Let me tell you something, ladies…neither your vagina nor vulva needs rejuvenating. Your labia are just fucking fine (pardon the pun). Once again, there are unscrupulous asshats out there preying upon women's insecurities and making bank in the process.

Labia and vulvas come in a wide variety of shapes and sizes, just like people do! There is nothing wrong with YOURS, and unless you've had an injury to the area (maybe from childbirth or cancer treatment such as radiation) or there's a melanoma or something else abnormal going on down there, you don't need any medical interventions. There are a lot of complications that are, frankly, not worth the risk in my opinion, including dryness, pain during sex, and skin that doesn't stretch (that's not a place where you want unstretchy skin, just sayin'!)

Don't even get me started on how much the beauty industry has made off women by trying to tell us we smell bad down there. Or that we need to be as smooth as a baby's bottom (just saying it that way makes it sound even more wrong!) A source I consulted said the Feminine Hygiene Products Market (which includes pads and tampons, but also cleansers, sprays, razors and blades) is expected to reach $42.7 billion by 2022 (https://www.alliedmarketresearch.com/feminine-hygiene-market).

In researching this chapter of the book, I also came across the concept of bleaching your vagina. WTAF, people? https://jezebel.com/your-vagina-isnt-just-too-big-too-floppy-and-too-hair-5900928

Seriously. That is fucked up, folks.

That women are somehow expected to be sexy 24/7 but also menstruate monthly, grow and deliver babies, and then go through menopause—it's all enough without having to worry about odor, bleaching, the length of our labia and the tightness of our vaginas, isn't it? Something has to give.

Basically, when you're working on all this body positivity stuff and learning to love your thighs and tummy, don't forget some love for your coochie too. Don't dismiss the effect that hormones can have on the way you feel and the way you feel about your body, either. And, guess what, you're going to get an opportunity to write your hoo-ha a love letter in the very next journaling assignment. Whoo-hoo!

Journaling Assignment #14: Lady Parts

You've probably just read the last chapter and are scratching your head. Maybe you're filled with dread about what I'm going to ask you to do next. I don't want you to panic, but I really do expect you to spend a little bit of time thinking about what it means to be female, and how that has impacted your view of your body through the years—and especially how those hormonal fluctuations affect the way you feel.

Maybe you'll write a manifesto promising to be kinder to yourself when those hormones are in flux. Maybe you just had a baby, and you're going to remind yourself that your body is still worthy of love, even if it looks different than it did pre-baby. Maybe you're going through menopause right now, and you have all sorts of thoughts and feelings you need to get out about how this new chapter of your life affects your identity and your body image.

All I can say is GO FOR IT!

THE FAT GIRL'S GUIDE TO LOVING YOUR BODY

SEX! (Yes, I'm Going There)— Oh, and Relationships

You didn't think I was going to just talk about vaginas and then leave you hanging, did you? Oh, no. I'm going to talk about sex and relationships right here, right now. Feel free to skip this chapter if you're celibate or asexual. Or too squeamish. I am not going to hold anything back.

Let's remember for a second that I write erotic romance under my other pen name, and I have a vast catalog of sexual experiences. I also use the hashtag #sexpositive to describe my erotic romance (in addition to #bodypositive). I think sex positive and body positive actually go hand in hand pretty nicely—because if you aren't ashamed of your body, you are a lot less likely to be ashamed of your sexuality.

I'm going to start off by saying something you may or may not know: many people of all genders are attracted to fat women. I don't mean they will tolerate a few extra pounds (and ugh, I remember seeing many a dating profile that bragged "I don't mind a few extra pounds." *Fuck yourself*, I wanted to say, *because I won't be!*) I mean they actually LOVE and PREFER fat women.

This is where it gets tricky, because even though there are plenty of folks who love and prefer fat women, not all of them are on the up and up. *What in the world are you getting at, Krista?*

Some people who prefer fat women are actually guilty of fetishizing them. I ran into this a lot when I was dating, during the time I was separated from my first husband. I could always tell when it was headed in that direction because all the guys' messages would have to do with my weight. If nearly all of their compliments and focus are on your size, there's a good chance fat is a fetish for them. If they don't seem interested in you as a person, what you do for a living, your family, background, hobbies, what you like to do for fun—if they only see you as a fat girl, then it's time to move on. If there's one thing you've learned from this book so far, it's that you're *greater than the sum of your parts*, and you have an identity way beyond your size or shape. Anyone you partner up with should understand that too!

Then you have the closeted fat girl lovers. These are the ones who want to see you in private and want to have sex with you, but they don't want to take you out on dates in public or introduce you to their friends or families. It might be that they're ashamed of your body, but more likely, they're ashamed of the fact they love your body, and they don't know what their circle will think about that. This is not okay. If you fall into a relationship where it feels like you never go out in public, and you've never met any of the person's friends or family, you need to confront your lover and ask why. You are a gem, my dear reader, and you should not be hidden away. PLEASE don't allow that to happen to you.

There's also this horrible trend of "pull a pig." I am not even going to dignify it with an explanation—you can Google it if you don't know what it means. It's cruel and inhumane. And if ANYONE thinks fat people aren't bullied, this is one example that definitively proves it.

It can be very difficult because so many women have been taught that they aren't desirable at their size, or that they shouldn't be having sex. So to have someone who is really into your body can be refreshing and validating, flattering, even. But you are worth so much more than being objectified like that. You deserve a partner who, yes, loves your body, but one who also loves your mind and heart.

You could also have a partner who dismisses your fatness, and that's not a healthy thing either. If you say something about being fat, and your partner says, "You aren't fat; you're beautiful!" you need to give him or her a big-ass eye roll because those two things are NOT mutually exclusive. Same thing if your partner dismisses your concerns that people sometimes treat you poorly because of your weight. Your partner needs to understand that living in a fat body means you're subjected to discrimination, and he or she should not invalidate your experiences.

On the opposite end of the spectrum, you could have a partner who ridicules you for your weight and fat-shames you. Has your partner made disparaging comments about your size? Have they outright asked you to go on a diet or insinuated you should?

I'm going to be super freaking honest with you. My husband has, in the past, made some rude comments about my size. The thing is, though, that he's overweight himself, and he has NOT discovered body positivity (though I preach it to him all the time!) He regularly fat-shames himself, and he's very caught up in the good food/bad food trap. I am really hoping he will read this book (*of course, then he'll get mad that I'm writing this, but this is my story. If he wants to write something and mention me, that's his prerogative!*), and maybe his mind will start to change. In any case, I know a lot of his feelings about my body are him projecting his shame about his own body onto me. We have talked about it extensively.

Let me tell you, though, unequivocally, you do NOT deserve to be shamed by your partner. Your partner should love you unconditionally, including your entire body.

I know very well how hard it is to leave a relationship, though, even one in which you're not being treated well or fairly. Without knowing you or your situation, I obviously can't give you specific relationship advice, but I can tell you that you deserve to be loved and treated well. I know sometimes we receive the message that fat people are less, that we are not worth as much as thinner people. But it's simply untrue.

If you're struggling in your relationship, I urge you to talk to someone. Friends are great, of course, but professionals are even better. You could go with your partner or go alone, or both. If you choose to go the professional route, definitely seek out a therapist who respects people of size and understands the kind of marginalization our community faces.

These next few paragraphs are mainly for my heterosexual cis-gender readers. I want to bring up something important here, and to be completely honest, it's something I've struggled with since my very first taste of male attention waaaaay back in junior high. I'm actually going to separate this out on its own line so it leaps off the page at you—that's how important it is:

You don't need a man to validate you!

Many women are taught that they're not complete if they don't have a man in their life. Or they're taught—even subconsciously—that their value is based on how attractive men find them. Remember what I've said again and again? **BEING PRETTY IS NOT YOUR JOB.** Likewise, you don't need male attention to confirm that you're attractive or desirable.

This is something I've struggled with, as I said, and I will fully admit when I first started my erotic romance pen name Instagram account and began to post photos in lingerie, I was incredibly flattered to accumulate so many male followers and to receive their likes and comments (not so much to receive their dick pics in my DMs. Unfortunately, that goes with the territory—though it shouldn't because I didn't consent to receiving those photos.)

It wasn't until the last year or so when I started to gain more female followers and had so many readers tell me that my photos were inspirational to them (I also got a lot of the *you're brave/you're so confident* crap I discussed earlier) that I realized showing my body so other women could see someone who looked like them on social media was my real purpose. I don't try to hide rolls or cellulite or stretch marks because it's important to show women *reality*, not some fantastical version of myself like advertisements and models do.

My hope is that I've been able to show fat girls that no matter their size, no matter their age, no matter their shape, they can still be sexy. And that you can dress in a way that's comfortable and sexy and helps you feel confident in your own skin. And, guess what? Feeling comfortable, sexy, and confident in your own skin is the best way to get yourself primed for sex or a relationship—or both, if that's what you want.

So, I want to assure you, in no uncertain terms, that you can and should have sex if you want to! (And *not* if you *don't* want to, of course!) There are certain positions that work better than others (lots of info is readily available if you search for it on the intrawebz), but the wonderful news is that plenty of fat chicks have really satisfying sex lives—and so can you.

If you ever doubt that fat girls can be desirable and sexy, I dare you to go to PornHub and take a look at the BBW section. Yeah, there are zillions of pornos out there featuring thick and plump girls of all sizes and shapes, and there are plenty of men and women who watch them.

So here's the moment you've all been waiting for: my sex advice for fat girls—really for anyone!

- Don't hide your body from your partner. Believe it or not, your partner—even if he or she has not seen you naked—already has a good idea of your size.

- Exude confidence. Not quite feeling it yet? Fake it till you make it. Trust me, people of all genders find confidence extremely sexy, and yes, there's a difference between confidence and cockiness.

- Wear something YOU feel amazing in. Doesn't matter if it's lingerie or a dress or boy shorts and a tank top. As long as YOU feel comfortable and sexy, it's perfect. And if you feel comfortable and sexy, the confidence thing will be a hell of a lot easier.

- Know your body. If you haven't intimately explored your own body, what the hell are you waiting for? Try some toys. Use your fingers. The time is now. If you don't know how to make yourself come, how do you expect anyone else to do it?

- Don't be afraid to laugh. Comical stuff can happen during sex—at least it does to me sometimes!—and it's totally fine to laugh. It will help you and your partner both relax.

- Penetration is not the end-all, be-all. The sexual smorgasbord is SO much bigger and more diverse than just penis-in-vagina sex.

- Be willing to experiment with positions. I know sometimes when we've been with one partner for a long time, we tend to gravitate to what we know works. But it's fun to spice things up with new stuff from time to time, right? Like I mentioned earlier, a simple internet search can yield some ideas about things to try. Just make sure you've recruited a friend to clear your search history if something ever happens to you. Or you could just OWN that shit like I do. *Hey, I'm a writer, so that's my excuse. *wink**

- Try not to focus on how your body LOOKS. Instead focus on how your body FEELS. Here's an example: instead of worrying about your breasts flattening and disappearing into your armpits (yeah, I went there LOL), think about how amazing it is when you partner kisses them or pays attention to your nipples. Concentrate on those sensations coursing through your body. *Spoiler Alert: that will put you in prime position to orgasm too!*

- Still having trouble forgetting how your body looks? Then focus on your PARTNER'S BODY and what you're doing to it. Is your partner a dude with a raging boner? Oh, yeah, that's for you, sis! You did that!

Journaling Assignment #15: Let's Talk About Sex, Baby!

You didn't really think I was going to let you off the hook journal-wise when it comes to this topic, did you?

This is for those of you who are or have been sexually active. If you're asexual or abstinent, feel free to skip this one.

I'd like you to reflect for a moment about what your sex life has been like as a fat girl up until this point (use extra sheets of paper if necessary, and if so, *you go girl!*) Then I want you to think about how you could improve it. Think about the advice I listed in the last section. How can you incorporate that advice? How does sex factor into your relationship(s), if you're in one—or more? Polyamory is a thing, you know!

THE FAT GIRL'S GUIDE TO LOVING YOUR BODY

Aging

What did Benjamin Franklin say? Something about the only certain things in life being death and taxes? Well, I would posit that aging is also a certainty, but I suppose it's also just the precursor to death. We now have longer life expectancies than nearly any other time in history (the exception being, of course, a few years ago—see this report from the Centers for Disease Control: bit.ly/FGGLink12).

In 1900, the average person met their Maker before their fiftieth birthday. Truly one of the most incredible advancements of the twentieth century—besides technology, of course—was the vast strides in lengthening life expectancy.

So our obsession with looking youthful past our forties, fifties, sixties, seventies—and beyond—is fairly recent because we didn't have a chance to become obsessed with looking youthful until we achieved a long life expectancy! It's pretty ironic when you think about it, no?

It's important to note that in third-world countries, a long life expectancy is not enjoyed like it is in developed countries. That makes our aversion to aging seem that much more shallow and vain, doesn't it?

Up until the past few decades, there was no market for age-defying diets, products, and advice because there weren't enough people getting old. But then the Baby Boomers came along, and now they are getting downright long in the tooth. While their parents were just thrilled to survive the Great Depression, Boomers are pretty used to getting what they want. No offense to any Boomers who might be reading this. (*My mom is a Boomer, by the way. I'm just a neglected and forgotten Gen Xer.*)

I don't need to go into the long and boring history of how we got to be so concerned with youthfulness. I don't think I'll hear any arguments from my readers that we are indeed fixated, if not completely and totally obsessed. We have a litany of cosmetic procedures, potions, creams, oils, etc. that all promise to make us look younger.

On the surface, I don't see anything wrong with wanting to look younger. Youth connotes greater vitality, increased energy—and most of all, more time to live, right? Because I think *that* is the hardest thing for us to come to terms with regarding aging. It means in no uncertain terms that our time is running out.

It was a trend in the past few decades to let women of a certain age fade into obscurity. Models simply vanished when they turned twenty-five or thirty. Actresses over forty had a hard time landing roles—there just weren't roles written for them. The entertainment, beauty, and fashion industries seemed to have collectively decided that older women (and by older, I mean younger than I am right now! Yikes!) were simply not attractive, worth looking at or hearing about.

I think we can thank the Boomer generation for turning the tide on this one. Even though we're still as obsessed with looking young as ever, celebrities such as Meryl Streep, Helen Mirren, Angela Bassett, Susan Sarandon, Viola Davis, Rita Moreno, Stevie Nicks, Jane Fonda, Dolly Parton, Alfre Woodard, and so many more are totally rocking it in their fifties, sixties and seventies.

So it's sort of a double-edged sword—because getting older is a given, and we seem to accept that, but there's this tremendous pressure to look great (read: younger) while doing it. So what does this have to do with fat girls, you ask? Well, not only do we have to worry about gray hair and wrinkles as we grow older, but it's often a time when our bodies change. We might gain weight. Our muscles might be less firm. We might develop wrinkles, varicose veins, saggy skin or age spots. There are a lot of physical changes that go along with aging that can cause us to spiral out of control with contempt for our bodies.

I'm writing this because I hope in your efforts to embrace your body as it is right now, you will condition yourself to continue accepting it as you age. If you're in your twenties or thirties, you might be like, "whoa, my body isn't so bad after all." But let me tell you, change, it is a'comin'! I was vaguely aware I was on the cusp of aging when I turned thirty or so, but I don't think the absolute imminence of it really hit me until the past couple of years. I have way more grays than I ever had before—though I'm still coloring the crap out of them (but more because I want to stay a redhead than anything else. My natural color is brown.) My joints ache a lot more than they ever did before. And my close-up vision is rapidly deteriorating. Though I don't wear them except to thread a needle, I did buy my very first pair of reading glasses in the last year. I can only imagine that their use will become more and more of a necessity in the coming months and years.

Yes, we can lose weight. We can exercise and get in shape. But one thing we cannot do is stop or reverse the aging process. It is happening whether we like it or not. So I suggest getting into the mindset that aging is a privilege denied to many, and you are incredibly blessed to receive the honor of growing old. Like I said at the beginning of this chapter, in third-world countries, life expectancy is a decade or two shorter than ours. So we are deeply privileged in our culture to live well into our seventies and eighties.

Do I think it's wrong to want to look your best as you age, meaning to hold on to your youthful looks as long as you can? No, I don't think it's wrong. Like I said, I color my hair. I've colored my hair since I was fourteen or fifteen, though, so the fact that it covers up the few grays I have at my temples and in my part is a bonus. I wear age-defying sunscreen products and makeup. I cover up the dark circles under my eyes almost every time I leave the house because when I don't, people ask if I'm sick or tired. I shouldn't care what they think. And hey, I *am* tired, that's no lie at all. But, *shrugs*, I still do it. I don't see anything wrong with it.

What is wrong, however, is the idea that we are past our prime after some arbitrary age like thirty or forty or fifty. We have a lot of vibrant living left to do at that point—decades of it! What's wrong is thinking a woman past X age is too old to have long hair or wear short skirts or be sexy. What's wrong is comparing yourself to younger women and allowing yourself to feel inferior or inadequate. Or disparaging your body as it goes through a completely natural (and as we discussed already: unavoidable) process. Or holding yourself to a set of beauty standards that can only be met by women in their late teens and early twenties.

As I've said many times already in this book: cut yourself some slack already! With age also comes wisdom, so I'm sure you're wise enough to understand that worrying about your age is only going to cause more wrinkles, right? (Hehe, that was a joke. *Sort of.*) Don't be ashamed of your age. Like your body, you should embrace it. It's as much a part of you as your body is. And, well, you have nowhere else to go, right?

Journaling Assignment #16: Aging Gracefully

Do you intend to age gracefully, or are you digging your heels in, endeavoring to look as young as possible for as long as you can? I'm not here to judge. I simply want to know how you plan to reconcile aging with this whole new bopo attitude you're (hopefully) sporting. Share below!

K.L. MONTGOMERY

Be A Good Role Model

Since we just spent all that time talking about aging, now is a good time to remember that there are future generations of women being born and raised as you read these words, and how we teach them to think about themselves will have a great deal of impact on how they actually do think and feel about themselves. So, here is some advice for being a good role model for your daughters, granddaughters, nieces, and any other young women in your life:

- Teach them it's not their job to be pretty.
- Don't put so much focus on looks. Compliment young women's minds, their ideas, moments when they're especially articulate, their problem-solving abilities, their artistic abilities, their athletic abilities, etc.
- Teach them that their worth lies in their hearts, minds, and souls. Not in their looks.
- Don't say disparaging things about your own body in front of young women. If you talk about your body at all, keep it positive.
- Don't say disparaging things about other people's bodies. Model an appreciation for diversity.
- Don't label young women's food choices as bad or good. Instead, teach them about nutrition and balance. Model the joy of eating, and yes, that means occasionally treating yourself to whatever you want with no guilt.
- Model a love for physical movement. Help young women discover ways to enjoy moving their bodies.
- Teach them not to look to others for validation.
- DON'T DIET. Look at any research about eating disorders—many patients report having had a mother who dieted. I know mine did when I was growing up.
- Don't comment on young women's bodies, especially not in a teasing manner.
- Model self-care. Teach them about self-care from a young age.

- Let them choose their own clothes. Don't judge their clothing choices, especially in terms of how their clothing fits their bodies/shape.
- Let young women know you're available to talk about any concerns they have regarding their bodies—and that you'll listen without judgment.

Journaling Assignment #17: Role Models

Reflect for a moment on whether or not you've had any body positive role models and how they helped shape your perception of your body. Then make a plan for empowering the young people in your life to treat their bodies with love and respect.

Your Diet is Not Just Food

I wanted to save this chapter for later in the book so you'd have a good foundation in body positivity before we tackled it. Though "diet" is a pretty bad word in this book (and the bopo movement in general), I want you to consider that your diet doesn't consist solely of the food you eat. Your diet consists of all the things you consume, and that includes messages received from people you know or encounter, entertainment, media, and social media.

We might not think what we're exposed to affects us that much. You might think you are aware that ads are photoshopped and airbrushed, and that much of what you see isn't "real." But the truth is that we construct our reality from all the messages and images we are bombarded with every day—it's not something that happens consciously. It happens in our subconscious.

When all you have seen represented is one very narrow standard of beauty, that is the exemplar you hold yourself up to. I know this to be true because once I began to fill my head with images of women who looked like me, ones who had thick thighs with cellulite and sagging boobs and bellies with stretch marks, the women began to look normal to me. I started to see beauty past all these things we've been told again and again are "unsightly." Remember what I said earlier about representation? It is SO true. And I'm going to prove it to you with these next two exercises.

During the next week or so, I want you to very closely examine what kinds of messages about bodies you're taking in and where they come from. In your journal, you can jot down the messages you received and where they came from: a person you know, a celebrity, a social media account, a movie, a TV show, the news, a song, a video, etc.

Examples:

Victoria's Secret ad where all the models have the same body type: tall, long limbs, thin and big boobs. Message: this is what sexy looks like.

A television show where a character is fat and is the punchline of every joke, the comic relief. Message: fat people aren't the main characters; they're just here to laugh at.

Friend's social media post celebrating a twenty-pound weight loss. Message: Losing weight is virtuous; gaining it is sinful.

Movie where the hero chooses the shy, unpopular, awkward girl over the hot cheerleader. Message: looks aren't everything.

At the end of the week, go through your list and note any negative messages. If it's from a person you know, consider your relationship with that person and whether or not you can limit the amount of time you're around them. If, for instance, you have a friend on a diet and she's constantly posting diet culture bullshit on Facebook, it might be time to unfollow her for a while. If you're following an Instagram account that posts "thinspiration" (*gag*), it might be time to unfollow it (permanently, I hope). Same with television shows or music. If you've been exposed to anything that hinders your bopo journey, I hope you'll consider eliminating it from your diet. (Oh yeah, in this case, you can *totally* eliminate stuff!)

Now, I want you to try something else. There are all sorts of body positive and fat acceptance accounts on social media. I know there are some on Facebook and Twitter, but where I really found the best sources of body positivity is Instagram. I am a HUGE fan! Not only do I have three accounts myself (one is for my puppy!), but I honestly believe I would not have gotten nearly as far on this body positive journey of mine without the amazing accounts I follow. What I'm going to do next is to give you a list of accounts to follow that I have found useful. It is by no means an exhaustive list, but it will definitely get you started. And once you start following these, it will start suggesting others like them.

You can start by following me: @k.l.montgomery

Note: these were all active at the time of writing. By the time you read this book, some of these accounts may have gone inactive. You can always search for more by using the hashtags #bopo or #bodypositive.

In no particular order:

@healthyisthenewskinny

@bodyposipanda

@yrfatfriend

@amysselflove

@win_the_diet_war

@aftermyownbelly

@fluffyfitandfabulous

@plussize_me

@plussize_universe

THE FAT GIRL'S GUIDE TO LOVING YOUR BODY

@rubyhooping

@londonandrews

@plussizepage

@bodyposirachel

@theabbybible

@thatnorachickonnyt

@ashleygraham

@comfyfattravels

@curvesbecomeher

@donutsoverdietculture

@tessholliday

@iamdaniadriana

@glitterandlazers

@yourstruelymelly

@thebodylovesociety

@thebodypositive

@i_weigh

@beyourjoy

@amyschumer

@benourishedpdx

@plussizecelebration

@therelatablefatgirl

@scarrednotscared

@with_this_body

@kristinabruce_coach

@your_body_is_good

@fatpositiveyaz

@fabuplus

@body_peace_liberation

@thefuckitdiet

@bodyimagemovement

@fatgirlflow

@effyourbeautystandards

@lizzobeeating

@theantidietplan

@theembodiedfatactivist

@positivebodyimage

@thebodyisnotanapology

And there are SO MANY MORE, but if you start an Instagram account and fill it with just these profiles, I guarantee you that in no time your feed will be filled with beautiful and inspirational fat chicks plus all the body positive messages you need to help your bopo mindset take shape. Like I said earlier, Instagram made a HUGE difference for me personally in my journey. It really does help to 1) constantly internalize body positive messages and 2) see other bodies that look like mine. We're not used to seeing fat or aging or regular bodies in entertainment or social media spaces, so it really is revolutionary to scroll through your feed and see a diversity of shapes, sizes and colors.

When Things Get Really Rough

No one knows better than me that things can't be sunshine, rainbows and unicorns all the time. Even though we want to be all bopo and in love with our bodies 24/7/365, I'm here to tell you, it's just not possible. There will be times when you look in the mirror or look down at your belly, your legs, or your arms, and you think, "I'm disgusting." That's why I've been so insistent that loving your body is a choice. It's one you will need to reaffirm every day. But some days, whether it's hormones or you're triggered by something in your environment, you're not going to love the skin you're in—you're going to loathe it.

And that's okay. It's okay because it's what you're feeling at that moment in time, and your feelings are *always* valid. But it's something you have to prepare for, and something you need to be willing to battle your way out of. Because if you let yourself sink into that deep, dark place I think we all have inside us, then you'll backslide and lose so much of the progress you've made toward loving and accepting yourself just the way you are.

I will be honest with you right now: I suffer from depression. It's a battle I've been fighting (and no, fighting is not too strong a word) since I was about twelve years old. I've undergone various treatments in the past thirty-some-odd years, but I haven't taken medication since I suffered a really horrendous bout of postpartum depression in 2000.

Small tangent, but still kinda relevant: I don't think there is anything wrong with taking medication to treat any illness. Taking an antidepressant isn't any different than taking insulin for diabetes, in my opinion. I have a few reasons I prefer to go the non-medication route for myself right now, but there are times I think I may be ready to try them again. The past few years, as I've been settling into this body positive mentality, have been rough for me depression-wise. Not because of anything to do with body positivity per se. I think a lot of it stems from my job. Being an author is fucking hard. And that's all there is to it. Writing the books is the easy part. The rest of it is a total roller coaster. But that's neither here nor there.

There are also times I miss my eating disorder days. I know it sounds really horrible to say that, and you're probably wondering what the hell is wrong with me, but hear me out. There is a certain type of manic high that can go along with starving yourself. I want to say I addressed this in *Fat Girl* when Claire talks about her eating disorder. There's a real sense of control and empowerment in starving yourself, in denying yourself. Why do you think people who eat such strict diets are so damn self-righteous? Because you really do feel like you have all things under control when you wrangle your stomach and cravings into submission. I miss that control sometimes.

But there's an inevitable crash. You slip up once, and everything crumbles around you. You feel like such a failure, such a fraud, and you know what you do most of the time? Not just jump right back on the bandwagon. Nope. You spiral out of control until you can somehow get the reins again. And then you start all over.

But what does all this have to do with you, you ask?

Because I've had some very, very low points in the past few years, I think I've gotten a lot better at identifying my triggers and helping guide myself out of the darkness. And I do think the self-awareness and the connection between body and mind that the body positive movement fosters helped a lot with that. Tell me if this sounds familiar: I can be coasting along, and everything's peachy keen, and then all the sudden BOOM, something will set me off, and I'll spend the next three or four days bursting into tears and so lethargic that all I want to do is sleep and eat sugar, which is exactly the worst thing I can do because it only makes me want more sleep and more sugar.

What happens when you're triggered depends a lot on your personality. For me, I want to crawl into a hole and not have any contact with anyone. I withdraw very deeply into my own mind, which fills with sick and twisted thoughts. I hate myself in those moments. I feel absolutely inadequate and worthless, like I will never be myself again.

Whether you've been diagnosed with depression or not, we all have ups and downs. If you do notice feelings of helplessness, hopelessness or any suicidal thoughts, PLEASE don't go it alone. Talk to someone you trust, and preferably a professional, about your feelings. I'll say it again: PLEASE! There is absolutely no shame in getting help with a problem, and, actually, if anyone should feel a sense of empowerment, it's someone who has gotten help with facing their depression. I remember back in college how scared I was to talk to my doctor about wanting to try an anti-depressant, but I'm so glad I did. I honestly don't know if I would still be around if I hadn't.

Okay, so that was my depression PSA, but back to my train of thought. Like I said, whether we have clinical issues or not, we all have ups and downs. I can't tell you what will work best for you; it may take some experimenting. But I implore you to identify your triggers and figure out how to head them off and take care of yourself. I'm going to share what works for me.

Identifying Triggers

So, first of all, what do I mean by identifying your triggers? Triggers can be anything from a smell, a sound, a sight, a memory, interactions with a certain person, anything that precipitates those really low feelings whether they manifest as full-blown depression, a panic attack, binge eating, binge drinking, or just a gloomy mood.

I'll tell you what mine are, and then I can share some more examples.

Probably the biggest trigger for me currently is book release days. I know, I know. It's supposed to be a happy occasion, and I'm supposed to be celebrating a huge accomplishment, but to me it's like I worked so hard, and then it's over. Usually my sales aren't as high as I'd hoped—they could probably never be as high as I hope, even if I try to manage my expectations. I had ten book releases in 2019, so I'm sure that is a big reason why I had so many episodes of depression.

Hormones are easily my second biggest trigger. I think I told you in the Female Issues chapter that I suffer from pretty horrible PMS, plus all the wonderful accoutrements like bloating, cramps, backache, migraines, fatigue and general bitchiness. The first thing I do when bad feelings start creeping up on me is look at the calendar to see if I'm due to start my period.

Another thing I have a hard time dealing with is really horrible things in the news, like mass shootings, for instance. I lose my hope in humanity and basically go to a deep, dark place. After the Sandy Hook shooting, I was just devastated. And after the Parkland, Florida shooting, I got the idea for my book *The Light at Dawn* and ended up writing it about nine months later. For the entire year after the Florida shooting, that book haunted me. I published it shortly before the one-year anniversary.

The final trigger for me is—okay, I'm just going to tell you—lack of sex or intimacy. Just ask my husband. If it's been a week or two, and I've had no physical attention, I am not a happy camper. I will spare you any other details, but it usually happens when he's on night work (he's a police offer, so he rotates from day shift to night shift every two weeks) and we hardly see each other, plus we're sleeping at opposite times. So that means half the month is ripe for neglect in that department—and it seems like one week of it always coincides with PMS. That's a recipe for disaster right there!

Okay, so those are MY triggers. Here are some others you might relate to:

- A snide comment about your weight from a friend or relative
- Being alone too much
- Being overwhelmed with too much to do
- The anniversary of traumatic events or losses
- Financial problems

There could be others as well. The trick is figuring out what they are. So, guess what, you're in a good position to do that because you've started to journal! And now that you've already completed seventeen journaling assignments (and you DID complete them, right? You better not be cutting corners!) you know how important it is and how well it works. So, this book ends with a daily body positive meditation for every day of the next year. As you're completing those each day, note your mood. When it drops and you feel yourself spiraling toward the darkness, ask yourself what is going on in your world that might have triggered it. Make a note of it in your journal.

Identifying Your Action Plan

Figuring out what your triggers are is only half the battle. After that, you have to figure out what will help stabilize your moods and help you feel good again. We often turn to things that, in the long run, are only going to make us feel worse. I said earlier I tend to crave and consume a lot of sugar, but if you know anything about the way sugar works on the brain and body (and I'm not saying it's a BAD food, only what it does to us chemically) you know that there are better choices. Maybe have just a little sugar, and then something to counteract that crash afterwards, like physical activity, okay?

Only YOU can figure out what your action plan is. But here is some food for thought, and I call it the Four Happy P's. When I visualize it, I see four tiny peas side by side in one pea pod with huge grins across their little animated faces. Yeah, I'm weird. Whatevs.

Explore the Four Happy P's to help you figure out what truly brings you joy. Then, when the time comes, immerse yourself in all those P's—and you'll feel some peace. See what I did there?

The Four Happy P's

1. *Happy Place*

    You've heard that one before, surely. Find your happy place! Oh, my, it's so true. I have a few happy places, and when I slip down into the deep, dark muck, I often visit one of my happy places to help pull me out of my depression. Some of my happy places are not very easily (or cheaply) accessed, so those must be saved for when time and finances allow (for example, Garden of the Gods in Colorado Springs and the entire city of Charleston, South Carolina). I try to have some local and semi-local places on the menu, though even *planning* a trip to one of the farther-flung locales can help boost your mood and give you something to focus on other than general ickiness (that's the technical term).

    My local and semi-local places include a walk down my road, which is out in the country and has fields and woods and is very peaceful, Assateague Island National Seashore (forty-five minutes from me), and Longwood Gardens in Kennett Square, Pennsylvania (we have an annual membership!)

    It doesn't even have to be an outdoorsy, nature-y place (though you can tell that's what I like). It could be the movies or the mall, or to the gym, or a certain coffee shop you like. One of my friends said the craft store was her happy place. Don't worry, you're going to get an opportunity to note your Happy Places (and the rest of your P's) in the next journaling assignment.

2. *Happy People*

    There are certain people who are just fun to be around and help lighten your mood. Or maybe there are people whom you trust and can lean on, who can help take some of the burden off you when you're feeling down. If you feel like being around people, being around your Happy People can help get you back on your feet again.

Probably my most important Happy Person is my son Kadan. He is an absolute joy—most of the time. He's also fourteen, so he can be moody once in a while. But usually he's a riot to be around, so clever and funny, you almost feel like you're at a stand-up comedy show the entire time you're with the kid.

I also have some writer friends I consider to be on my Happy People list. One is a writer I can turn to when I'm feeling down about my career because we have a lot of the same thoughts and feelings about the industry, and we can always commiserate. And I have a few other regular friends I can get in touch with when I'm feeling down. It's amazing to have people like that in my life. I hope you have some people like that too!

3. *Happy Passions*

Happy Passions are the hobbies and other fun activities you like to pursue that bring meaning and purpose to your life. Writing is a job for me these days, so I don't really include that on my list. Other things I enjoy that I would consider passions are seeing theatre and live music (especially Broadway and symphony orchestras), looking at art, going to museums, and traveling. I enjoy documentaries about science and history as well. I'm basically a big old nerd, so I find getting in touch with my inner nerd takes the focus off the crappy stuff weighing me down. Maybe you really enjoy painting, coloring books, knitting, or playing an instrument. It could be watching sports on television, rock concerts, video games or playing with your pets. Maybe your happy passion is exercise—more power to you, if it is!

4. *Happy Pleasures*

Happy pleasures are the indulgent self-care type things we enjoy that relax and soothe us. Maybe you like to get a massage or a facial. Perhaps you enjoy getting a manicure or pedicure. Maybe a bubble bath is a happy pleasure for you. Maybe it's a good old-fashioned orgasm (delivered by yourself or a partner, either way!) If you are a neat and tidy sort of person, you may get a lot of pleasure out of reorganizing your closet. I can't personally identify with that one, but hey, I'm not going to judge, okay?

We're going to talk more about self-care and how important it is in the next chapter.

So are your wheels starting to turn? Hopefully between those four different areas, you are starting to develop your own action plan should you go into crisis mode. There could be other avenues to explore as well. If you're a spiritual person, you may find praying or meditating helps you cope. Or if you're really digging this journaling thing, doing a free-write where you just pour out everything on your heart and mind might be cathartic. It may take some experimentation to figure out the best way to get yourself back on track if you slip into the deep, dark abyss.

If you find that your low mood has crossed the line into what you think might be depression, or if it begins to interfere with your ability to work or maintain relationships, please strongly consider seeking professional help. I know it takes a lot of courage to do that, but you're worth it! You're worth fighting for. <3

Journaling Assignment #18: Identifying Triggers & Action Plan

We just talked about what to do when we go into crisis mode. The first step is to figure out what causes our drop in mood. These are called triggers, and I outlined a few of my own and other common ones in the prior chapter. It may take some time and reflection to figure out what yours are, but if you have some ideas, jot those down now.

Then think about The Four Happy P's we discussed a few moments ago. These are your Happy Places, Happy People, Happy Passions, and Happy Pleasures. Make a note of them below and begin to think about what your action plan might look like. Also consider if your regular routines or your relationships are disrupted enough by low mood that perhaps it's time to seek help from your doctor or a therapist.

K.L. MONTGOMERY

Self-Care

Self-care is a term I learned when I started following bopo folks. If you aren't aware, it's anything we do to take care of our minds, bodies, or spirits. In other words, it can encompass a lot of different things. A lot of people think about the "Happy Pleasures" part of The Happy P's I discussed in the last chapter when they think of self-care, but it's really a lot broader than manicures, pedicures, bubble baths and massages—though those things certainly could be self-care.

First, we have to talk about how damn important it is! We are so insanely busy these days—and much of our "busy-ness" involves taking care of other people or things. Most of us have jobs workin' for "The Man,"—or working for ourselves, which is what I do—and there are lots of responsibilities and stress that come with work. And many of us have families, and whether we are taking care of our partners, children, pets, parents or other loved ones, a lot of times the bulk of domestic responsibilities falls on women's shoulders (which sucks, but, hey, it's true, even if it's old-fashioned and kind of sexist. I do think it's improving, but we have a long way to go in that regard, don't you think?) Anyway, suffice it to say, we have a lot of things on our plates, and sometimes we forget to claim a little wedge on that plate for ourselves. We should actually have a good-sized wedge, but the first item on our to-do list we tend to push aside is taking care of ourselves.

Multiple studies have shown that neglecting your own emotional, mental, and physical needs can have adverse effects. It can lower our moods and productivity while increasing our anxiety and potential for getting sick. What makes it even more challenging is that only YOU can make sure you're doing it for YOURSELF. You have to make the time and not make excuses, which can be hard when you have toddlers vying for your attention, or a project due, or bills that need to be paid. I implore you to carve out some time, though, maybe even a few minutes a day most days, peppered with longer sojourns, even entire weeks or weekends if you can spare it.

Here's a little bit of a spoiler alert: a lot of self-care focuses on your body, so practicing it will foster some major body love. And even the stuff that focuses on your mind is STILL good for your body too, 'cause they're connected and stuff!

Here are some ideas ranging from the simplest and least time-consuming to the grandest, longest, and most indulgent (but obviously would pay huge dividends, right? Also, if your partner is on the fence about funneling time and resources into this self-care thing, you can show them this list and say Krista told you to do it. So there!)

1. Get some freakin' sleep! Aim for seven to eight hours a night. And naps are a wonderful thing if you can manage to sneak some in from time to time (maybe a George Costanza-esque nap desk is in order? Hey, that might be my first *Seinfeld* reference of the book! Probably not my last, though.)

2. Spend time with your loved ones—quality, relaxing time where you're doing something fun, of course!

3. Eat something you enjoy without feeling guilty—or bad. Please don't feel bad about anything you eat.

4. Just say NO! Learn the fine art of saying no to things that are too overwhelming, too stressful, or not worth your time or energy. Set boundaries with people so you can concentrate on what's really important.

5. Engage in physical activity—that's why so many of the bopo meditations that follow the main part of this book involve movement of some kind. You really are taking care of yourself when you move your body like it's designed to do.

6. Meditate/reflect/pray. Not sure if you've heard, but there are literally 365 bopo meditations at the end of this book. Yes, you're supposed to journal them, but you could also sit and contemplate them. Or you could just wipe your mind of every single thing, concentrate on your breathing, release any tension your body is holding, and just BE for a few moments.

7. Spend some time in nature. Vitamin D is a super amazing thing that your body NEEDS and CRAVES. Also, being in nature, even if it's in your own back yard or the neighborhood park is restorative and helps put everything in perspective.

8. READ! (I am obligated to say this as an author.) It doesn't have to be a novel (though if you do like novels…I know someone who writes body positive ones, just sayin' *wink*) It could be an interesting article on the internet or a good old-fashioned magazine. Reading rocks!

9. Animals!!! Animals are great for relieving stress, and you don't even have to actually own one. Yes, you could pet your dog or cat—or you could even just watch silly cat videos or smile at adorable puppy pictures.

10. Limit your screen time. Unplug! You don't need to have your phone or computer on 24/7, you know. You can turn your ringer off and shut your laptop and go pretend it's 1975 or even 1875 if you want (I sure hope I'll listen to this one myself!)

11. Practice one of the Happy Passions you listed in the last journaling assignment. You don't have to be at your wit's end to pursue a Happy Passion, you know. You can make it part of your regular routine as well.

12. Have an orgasm. Not even kidding you—this is really the ultimate in self-care, and it's absolutely free. Use a toy, use your imagination, or get a partner on board.

13. Put on a face mask, take a hot bubble bath or a nice long shower, or shave your legs. Whatever you find relaxing. Just 15-20 minutes of solitude in your very own bathroom. See? Simple and cheap!

14. Have more time and money? Plan a spa day. Get a massage or a mani/pedi. Get a professional facial.

15. Two words: retail therapy. If you love to shop, you know what I mean. Buying yourself something pretty (a new dress, a new shirt, new shoes, a handbag, jewelry, a scarf, even just a bottle of nail polish in a color you love) can feel pretty damn good, and it doesn't have to cost that much. Retail therapy is one of my personal favorite forms of self-care.

16. One word: VACATION! So, the ultimate form of self-care is taking a vacation. You could do a *staycation* if funds are tight, but I am a big believer in travel for so many wonderful reasons. It opens up your mind and heart, and exposes you to people, places and ideas that you could never fully appreciate in a book or movie.

    You don't have to go far, necessarily, though sometimes it's fun to save up and take a trip someplace super awesome. In the past few years I've done a lot of traveling for book signings, which is always fun, but I also made time for a few real vacations and those destinations have included Disney World (okay, not the most relaxing itinerary, but wow we had a blast), Colorado, Montreal, Niagara Falls, and New York City.

Journaling Assignment #19: Make a Plan for Self-Care

The thing about self-care is that it needs to be deliberate. You have to make time to practice self-care. So based on the ideas I just gave you, expound here about how you will find time for self-care. Try to list things you will do every day, things you will do weekly, things you will do monthly and things you will do once a year (like a vacation or a girls-only road trip, for example.) You could probably even count doing this journal entry as self-care!

Dressing Your Body

I polled my readers in my Facebook group about whether there were any items of clothing they refused to wear due to their weight or shape, and here were some of their answers:

- Short skirts
- Short sleeves
- Tank tops
- Shorts
- Leggings
- Two-piece bathing suits
- Capri pants
- Rompers
- Tight shirts
- Dresses

Um, I'm not sure if you had the same thought as me, but if you refused to wear any of these things, what the hell WOULD you wear? A burlap sack? I hate the fact that so many women have been made to feel like their bodies aren't worthy of certain types of garments. When you put it like that, it sounds so ridiculous, right? They're just clothes. As long as your private parts are covered up and you're warm enough, what the hell difference does it make what skin is showing?

I've had my own fashion-related battles throughout the years, which I'm going to rehash shortly, but as I'm telling my story, think about your own. What did you like to wear when you were younger that you feel like you could no longer get away with wearing now because of your size or age? You know all of those rules are completely arbitrary and meaningless and have more to do with other people's hang ups and insecurities than actual fat bodies, right?

If you spend any time looking at my Instagram accounts, it will probably be rather apparent I'm a bit of a clothes horse. I actually had to look that phrase up to make sure it's actually a thing and not something I made up, though I'm not sure why anyone would compare themselves to a clothed horse. Anyway, it's a thing. It means someone who is into fashion, basically.

I've always enjoyed shopping and clothes. I will be perfectly honest that it was a lot easier to find the kinds of clothes I liked when I was younger and straight-sized. I could waltz into almost any store and find my size, and they usually fit pretty well off the rack too.

After I had my first son, it was my first time having to wear plus-size clothes. I'd been a size fourteen before he was born, which meant I could shop almost anywhere. But after he was born I was a twenty-two. And that was back in the late nineties when there were hardly any choices for plus-size clothing at all. There were Lane Bryant and Cato's. That's about it where I lived in central Indiana. The department store plus-size departments were so matronly and dowdy—and I was in my early twenties when I became a mother.

The first time I went shopping after he was born and had to buy a size twenty-two, I thought I would die. I was so disheartened, so embarrassed, and so defeated. I had this beautiful baby boy, but I also had a body that didn't feel like home anymore. I was like, *who the fuck is this chick?* Every time I looked in the mirror, there was a serious disconnect.

That is probably what triggered my old eating disorder to flare up. I lost eighty pounds in nine months after Tristan was born. I was eating anywhere from six hundred to twelve hundred calories a day and exercising for hours. Is it any wonder I had to wean him? I couldn't produce enough breast milk under those conditions. And I've already told you how I gained all the weight plus some back again with the next baby (though that was also after suffering three miscarriages, and I often wonder if I jacked up my hormones through starving myself, and that's how I developed luteal phase defect.)

After Jordan, son #2, I wasn't as uncomfortable in my body as I was before, but I was so tired. So. Damn. Tired. Jordan didn't sleep. Like I said in the crisis mode chapter, I battled postpartum depression. So I was lucky if I was even dressed, let alone in something cute.

It wasn't until after Kadan, son #3, arrived in 2005, and my third round of shopping in plus-size stores that I really started to embrace plus-size fashion. It helped immensely that other stores were starting to expand their size selections. Even discount retailers like Target and Wal-Mart were getting better about their offerings.

And then I discovered Torrid. It wasn't until probably 2012 or 2013, but once I tried on a few things and subsequently bought them, it was like someone had a mannequin molded from my body and then designed clothes for it. Now probably 75-80% of my wardrobe comes from Torrid.

I guess this long diatribe is basically to point out that it took me from 1997-2013'ish to really find what worked for me as a plus-size woman. Granted, I spent several years of that wearing a size 14 or 16, which meant I could shop a lot of other places. But now that I'm in the 18/20 camp, it's Torrid all the way for me. The gist is you have to figure out what works for you.

There are tons of places to buy plus-size clothes now. I still get some things from Lane Bryant, some from Old Navy, Target, Cato's, and some department stores, most of which have a plus-size department now (and they're not always the matronly clothes of the past, either). In addition, there are a ton of online clothing stores that offer plus sizes or even cater to plus sizes such as Eloquii, Simply Be, Fashion to Figure, and Dia & Co, which is a subscription service. I haven't tried all of those yet (I'd have to funnel some money away from my Torrid obsession—and no, sadly, I'm not getting any kickbacks from this huge endorsement!)

So the other part of what I want to say here is that YOU ARE WORTH LOOKING GOOD. And I don't mean pretty or thin. I mean GOOD—whatever GOOD means to you. Whether your style is casual, dressy, sporty, romantic or trendy, there are definitely stores out there with clothes that will suit both your tastes and your body. The trick is trying on a LOT of stuff. The old adage, "you have to kiss a lot of frogs before you find your prince" should really be "you have to try on a lot of jeans before you find a pair that fits—and you like."

One thing I would throw out completely are the unfair and arbitrary fashion rules that are fatphobic and discriminatory. Things like fat women shouldn't wear horizontal stripes or loud prints or bright colors or two-piece bathing suits or shorts. FUCK THAT. One of the things I love about the new plus-size stores is that they make every style, and you can almost undoubtedly find it in your size.

Basically, in answer to your question of how you dress your fat body, I say "put clothes on it." I know, it sounds flippant, but I say that because I'm sick and tired of fat women thinking they have to dress in monotone colors or all black or cover up their bodies. You have just as much right to wear what you want as any skinny chick. Wear what you love. Wear what you feel good in. It's so liberating to just dress for yourself and give a total of zero fucks what anyone thinks about it.

Trust me on this. It took me many years to get to this point, and I have been both body-shamed and slut-shamed for my clothing choices my entire life. I finally realized a few years ago that clothes just look different on me because of the way I'm shaped. I have a ginormous rack, okay? I can't help it if I show cleavage. Like even in a slight V-neck t-shirt, I show cleavage. The girls are just there, alright? I'm not wearing a turtleneck so you can avoid seeing that I have mammary glands that like to get cozy with each other.

And leggings. It took me a while to embrace leggings because I have very thick thighs and an ample butt. But after wearing them a few times and seeing how comfortable they are, I am now of the opinion that if you don't like it, don't look. It's as simple as that. My job is not to make you comfortable with my clothing choices. My job is to make ME comfortable with my clothing choices.

And wearing a two-piece bathing suit on the beach in all my fat glory? Well, it's pretty empowering, I'm not going to lie. The more you push your boundaries, the less you will care what others think. Please take this advice to heart. It really makes all the difference to just be yourself and not worry about judgment from others.

And speaking about judgment from others…that's what we're going to talk about next. Only not just judgment FROM others but TOWARD others as well.

Journaling Assignment #20: Fashion Going Forward

How would you describe your style at the moment? Where do you shop? What type of clothes do you typically wear?

Contrast that with what you'd LIKE to be able to wear and where you'd LIKE to try shopping. Then, I hate to go all Nike on you, but just do it!

It Costs Nothing to Be Kind, But It Does Take Some Work

We are wired to make snap judgments; did you know that? Being able to make snap judgments and inferences protected early humans from peril. For example, if we or a loved one from our tribe had a nasty run-in with a snake, we'd be wary of all snakes, and as soon as we encountered one, our fight or flight reflex would kick in. Maybe it wasn't a snake but a lion. Or a shark. Or a poisonous toad or mushrooms. Early humans had a lot to be afraid of. It was them against nature, so our big ol' brains evolved to make snap judgments.

Today we use those skills to decode what kind of person someone is purely by the way they look. It is almost impossible to keep your brain in neutral mode when you meet someone and wait to get to know them before judging them. Whether it's racial and ethnic prejudice, the inkling (get it?) that someone covered in tattoos must be a criminal, or fear that a man bearing a mustache (who isn't Tom Selleck) is probably either a 70s porn star or a child molester…we almost instantly categorize people purely based on appearance.

Don't believe you make snap judgments? Okay, I'm going to give you an archetype, and as soon as you read each description, I want you to close your eyes and see if you can conjure up a mental image of that person immediately.

- *A biker chick*
- *A businessman*
- *A Superhero*
- *A PTA Mom*
- *A nerdy guy*
- *A goth girl*
- *A librarian*

Well, how did you do?

So, while this ability to make snap judgments in the past was a boon to human survival, we don't exactly face the same challenges today than we did thousands of years ago. When someone thinks of "fat girl," what do you think they conjure up in their minds?

They might think of someone who is slovenly, unkempt, lazy, ugly, awkward.

Is that a fair assessment?

Is that what *you* look like?

It's probably not the way you would describe yourself. This ability leads to a lot of unkindness and prejudice, not to mention the well-documented fear of "the other." That's where we dehumanize people who are different from us because we have an irrational fear and, thus, hatred of them. In many ways, that's what fatphobia is all about. In some people's very small minds, becoming fat is the worst fate imaginable. And when they look at fat people, that fear comes out in a horribly demeaning way.

But we *all* have our own prejudices and fear of "the other." We cannot be touting body positivity and shouting from the rooftops for fat acceptance if we harbor hate and prejudice against others.

That's why I want to spend a few moments talking about kindness. It's such a simple, simple concept isn't it? Did your mother ever teach you the Golden Rule when you were growing up? The one that says "Treat other people the way you want to be treated?" I know mine harped on this concept quite a bit—and as a primary school teacher for thirty years, I am sure she said it in the classroom hundreds or thousands of times throughout the course of her career.

Why is it *so* hard to treat other people the way we want to be treated, especially when it *sounds* so simple?

Well, like I said, we are hardwired to make snap judgments, and it's either innate, or we're taught very early on to have an irrational fear of "the other." So in some ways we're fighting off some very primal urges when we try to avoid classifying people before we actually get to know what they're about, when we try to refrain from judging them by their appearance.

Want to see how prevalent the problem is? Go to Wal-Mart, yes Wal-Mart (other stores would work too, but Wal-Mart is hands down the BEST for this experiment). Study every single person who comes into view. That mom with the four loud kids. That fat couple loading their cart down with junk food. That man whose cart is full of beer. The woman wearing pajama bottoms and riding around on an electric cart with cigarettes in the basket. Hell, you probably didn't even have to see them in person. You probably judged them just from reading my comments. But, seriously, go to Wal-Mart and try to see these people and NOT judge them. Instead, tell yourself "There's a person who is at Wal-Mart because they need groceries or household items, just the same as me. We're the same. We're both shopping in Wal-Mart to buy some things we need for ourselves or our families."

Now think about how both types of thought patterns made you feel.

I'm going to go out on a limb and say that the second thought pattern engendered much stronger feelings of positivity than the first.

We are wired to spot the differences between ourselves and people and not the similarities.

Can you imagine how different our world would be if we were wired to spot sameness instead of otherness?

I saw a sign outside a church the other day that really resonated with me. It said, "There is no 'other.' There's only 'us.'" What a beautiful sentiment!

So, what does this have to do with kindness and body positivity, you ask? I was hoping I wouldn't have to spell it out for you, but I will anyway. It is MUCH easier to be kinder to someone—and to treat them the way you want them to treat you—if you see them as similar to you instead of different.

Kindness is possibly the most underrated quality in the entire spectrum of human personality traits. It's just not as valued as intelligence, wit, determination, boldness, or leadership abilities. I wish we valued it above beauty, for sure. And it would be fantastic if it bumped a few of the other traits I mentioned down the totem pole. Our world would be a much nicer place to live in if we all practiced kindness.

I want to challenge you to look inward and think about whether or not you are a kind person. Please note: being kind *doesn't* mean being a pushover. It *doesn't* mean letting others take advantage of you. On the contrary, setting boundaries and limits for people is often a very kind thing to do, especially when they are enforced with kindness and love.

I will be the first to admit I have a rather snarky inner voice that delights in making snap judgments about people I see out in public or in online spaces. When I spot a grammar faux pas, for instance, I have to literally bite my tongue! I am slowly learning to quiet that inner snarky voice. It says a lot more about me when I have cruel or unkind thoughts about someone than it says about them. It speaks to my own unhappiness, my own insecurities.

Part of the body positive movement is learning to be happy in one's own skin and to shed one's insecurities, so the need for that snarky judgy voice inside my head keeps diminishing. I now try to purposely fill my head with kind and positive thoughts when I'm out and about. It can be SO hard—like I said, even though it sounds so simple. But here are some examples:

The woman in the pajama bottoms on the electric cart at Wal-Mart? I might wonder if she's been sick or struggling with depression. Lord knows I can relate to the depression thing. Maybe she did her very best to get out of the house today.

The woman with the four young, very loud kids, some people would automatically think "There's a bad mom who can't control her children. She needs to learn what birth control is for." Isn't that mean? But, come on, you know a lot of people would think that, maybe even you. But I try to think something along the lines of, "Wow, I remember how hard it is to shop with a bunch of kids in tow, and she has one more to deal with than I ever had. I bet she's doing the best she can. She probably needs a spa day or to do something nice for herself!"

People often quote that it costs nothing to be kind. It's true that it's free in a monetary sense, but it does take a lot of willpower and training your brain. I challenge you to work on this. I know it sounds crazy, but when you start being kind to others, it's also easier to be kind to yourself—and vice versa, I think. Kindness begets kindness. Not only will you treat yourself better, but the people you are kind to will often pay it forward, multiplying your effort exponentially.

Journaling Assignment #21: My Pledge to Be Kind

This might feel like something you did in kindergarten when you were first learning how to get along with people you aren't related to. It may feel silly to make this kind of pledge as an adult. But I want you to write a statement about how you plan to incorporate kindness into your life, to embrace it and make it something you are known for. You'll notice in the bopo meditations at the end of the book that several are related to kindness and relationships with other people. That's because it's too important to ignore. So write your pledge, and be specific about how you will work on it, and how you will stay accountable. And then DO IT!

Building Your Tribe

You've come this far, and you're almost to the end of the journaling assignments and the meat (or the tofu for my vegetarian/vegan readers) of this book. You may feel like you've learned a lot already. I definitely hope you have! Now is the part of the book where I tell you that you'll be a lot more successful on your bopo journey if you build a tribe of like-minded folks and people you can lean on for support. Hopefully those folks will be one and the same.

Why do you need a tribe?

- Accountability. If you've set goals for kindness or journaling or movement every day or whatever (just please not dieting or restricting calories), then it's always nice to have someone to check in with and hold you accountable, preferably someone who will metaphorically kick your ass if you get off track.

- Celebration. If something exciting happens in your life—a new baby or grandbaby, a promotion, a marriage, etc., it's always good to have people who are genuinely happy and excited for you to celebrate with. And you can be there to celebrate their achievements with them, too. Because who doesn't love a party, right? Life would be so dull without them.

- Commiseration: Not that you're going to be miserable—at least I hope you won't be, but you will have down days, and when you do, it's nice to be able to confide in someone who understands what you're going through. If you're having a day where you really hate your body, being able to call up a friend to tell them about your feelings is priceless. Maybe they will tell you to go enjoy nature or to practice some self-care. Maybe they'll let you cry on their shoulder. In any case, it's always a plus to have a friend to turn to when you are down or in crisis mode.

- People who really GET you. Maybe you have a quirky sense of humor. Maybe you have a geeky passion that others just don't understand. Maybe you have a potty mouth and need to be around others like you. Whatever idiosyncrasies you have, it's important to have people in your life who you can truly be your genuine self around, where you don't have to put on any airs and can let down your hair, so to speak.

Where do you find these people, pray tell?

That's a good question. I personally have had a lot of trouble in my life with female friendships, and I'll be perfectly up front about it. I could tell you horror stories about all the times I've been thrown under the bus by women who were supposed to be my friend, but I'll spare you the gory details. It's SO HARD, especially as an adult, to make friends. Especially for someone like me who works from home and can go days without seeing humans other than my husband, sons, and the mail carrier (she's a woman, at least, yay!)

I could probably write an entire book about female friendships, but I have fiction books to get back to after this one, so I better shelve that idea for later. Suffice it to say that I understand how hard it is. Most recently, my most reliable and satisfying friendships have all been conducted online. Sometimes these friendships are with people I might never meet in "real life." Though I would argue that many online spaces are as much like real life as actual real life, but I digress.

So here are at least some things to consider when it comes to building your tribe. Even though I can't tell you exactly how to find yours, I can tell you you need one.

- What are your passions? Look for your tribe in those spaces, whether they are online forums or cooking classes or local volunteer efforts. If you're a reader, a book signing is a great place to meet kindred spirits in person, I can attest to that! If you're a spiritual person, you may find your tribe at church or some other fellowship. If you're a gamer, you might find your tribe in a virtual space or playing Dungeons & Dragons at the local comic book store. There are a zillion Facebook groups for every passion or background you can dream of. For example, I recently joined a large group for women who are married to police officers. Even though there are thousands of members, it's a very tight-knit community, and I already get the impression that they'd do almost anything to help support a fellow member.

- Be yourself. You're only going to attract the right people if you're presenting your genuine self to them.

- Be open-minded. The best tribemate may not be a woman your age who looks like you and has a similar background. It may be someone older or younger. It may be someone in a different life stage, or who has children whereas you don't (or vice versa). It could be a man! Some of my best friends in the world are men. I tend to get along with men better than women, and I don't have any horror stories about male friendships. And, believe me, you CAN have a platonic friendship with someone of the opposite sex.

- Vet people before you get too close. I wish I didn't have to say that, but not everyone has good intentions, as I'm sure you know. You're looking for people who are going to root for you, so at the first sign of jealousy, you should move on. Watch how your potential tribemates treat others. Are they kind? Genuine? Truthful? If not, kick 'em to the curb. Those aren't the droids you're looking for. (And there you have it, my pathetic attempt at a *Star Wars* joke!)

- On the other hand, don't stay closed off too long. Your tribe will be made up of people you need to be able to open up to. Be honest about where you're coming from and your feelings. If you have negative feedback for your tribe member, don't hold back, but be gentle and kind. Ask that they are also honest with you. There is definitely a degree of vulnerability that goes into being part of a tribe, but if the tribe is strong and supportive, your vulnerability will be rewarded.

- Nurture your tribe by doing stuff together, even if it's virtually. I mean, the ultimate thing would be a girls' night out or some sort of trip together. But even just checking in with friends via text or private message on social media can go a long way toward maintaining a friendship. I have lost more than one friendship because I always seemed to be the one reaching out. It takes two to tango, ya know what I mean?

- Give as good as you get. This goes beyond the reaching out/nurturing advice above. If you really want your tribe to be there for you in thick and thin, you need to do the same for them. Don't always be the one in crisis. You need to have strong shoulders for your tribemates, and you need to be just as willing to stand up and cheer for them when they are celebrating a milestone.

We all crave that feeling of belonging, of being part of something that's bigger than just ourselves, and tribes provide that sense for us. It hearkens all the way back to when humans really did live in tribes—I mean, that's where the concept comes from, right? There is a lot of power in a small group of like-minded and interconnected people. Use that power for good. Once you're established, consider how your tribe can make a positive influence on the world.

Journaling Assignment #22: Building Your Tribe

If you guessed I was going to make you journal about building your tribe, then *ding ding ding*, you are correct! Do you already have a tribe? Explain who it is and what it's about. Still searching? Jot down some ideas on how to find your tribemates. You can also elaborate on what specifically you'd like to get out of your tribe and what you feel you have to contribute.

Your Official Invitation to Join My Fat Girl's Tribe!

Hey, what do you know, dreams DO come true! I'm extending a heartfelt invitation to join the tribe I've recently created on Facebook. It's a group format, and right now I'm the only admin, but once the community grows (fingers crossed that will happen once this book is out in the world), I plan to add some more volunteers so we can make it a safe, vibrant, and accepting community where we can share in bopo success stories and encourage each other when the going gets tough.

Right now, I've been posting lots of memes, articles, videos, questions and inspiration related to body positivity. Most of the members currently come from my romance reader fan base, and I can tell you right now there are some amazing ladies there just waiting to welcome you with open arms! We'd love to have you on board.

It's very simple to join. Simply navigate to https://www.facebook.com/groups/FGGLYB/.

Three questions will pop up, and make sure you answer them fully, or I won't be able to accept your membership. I am limiting this to women only, and I want to make sure it's ladies who are committed to learning to love their bodies. No judgment or shaming of any kind will be tolerated. I want it to be an open and positive space where we can all learn and grow together.

I can't wait to see you there!

But wait, there's more!

Did you ever watch those silly infomercials for As Seen On TV products? I feel like I've reached that point in this book. I've poured my heart and soul into this, but before I go, I want to say a little bit about how I got the idea for this book, and share my hopes and dreams for my own bopo journey.

I just searched my email to make sure on the date, but apparently it was September 6, 2019, at approximately two o'clock in the afternoon while I was waiting in the pick-up line at my youngest son's high school that the idea for this book came to me. You have to get there early to get a good spot, which means you have thirty or forty minutes of quiet contemplation—or time to fool around on social media. I was sitting there, and I don't even know what I was doing or thinking about, but suddenly the idea for this book popped into my head. I opened up the notes app in my phone and scrambled to get all the ideas in my head onto the screen, and then I promptly emailed myself the document. The outline for this book came from that email, and it's almost exactly the same as I originally envisioned. All I did was add the journaling component and a little more material.

In the past few years, I've had so many women, many of whom have been readers of my romance novels, tell me that I've inspired them to dress differently or see their body differently. I often hear that people "admire my confidence" or are "envious of my confidence." I already told you how I feel about being labeled as brave or confident. I don't really see myself that way because I still struggle with my body sometimes.

It's only when I look back to how I treated my body when I was younger that I really see how far I have come. I made a habit of starving myself. I can tell you at least five or six time periods in my life where I restricted my calories below 1200 a day. I can also attest to spending hours upon hours forcing myself to burn calories in the pool, on the elliptical, by jogging (with these boobs! Yes, it's a sight to behold LOL). I wasn't moving my body because I loved it; I was moving it to punish myself for the weight I'd put on. I wasn't eating for fuel or for enjoyment. I was eating the bare minimum necessary to keep my body functioning, and sometimes it just didn't function at all. I regularly experienced dizziness from low blood pressure and even passed out a time or two.

The needle on the scale controlled my emotions. If the needle went down, I was elated. If it went up, I was defeated. I was a slave to that number. My worth, my value, it was dependent on what that stupid rectangle I stood on every morning said. Sometimes more than just once a day. At the height of my eating disorder, I was weighing myself three or MORE times a day! Talk about obsessed!

And every time, I would gain back weight. As soon as I started to eat like a normal person again, I would pack the pounds back on. Every time I got another positive pregnancy test, I swear I immediately gained twenty pounds. And then I had to face the doctor admonishing me about my weight gain every time I went in for a check-up. What he didn't know was that my body was just trying to get back to where it wanted to be.

I don't believe everyone is meant to be thin. I don't believe there's a thin person inside every fat body just waiting to break out, and that whole notion disgusts me because it dehumanizes and devalues fat bodies. And if there's one thing we've learned about fat- and body-shaming it's that it does NOT motivate people to become skinny. Quite the opposite, in fact.

I knew when I wrote *Fat Girl* in 2015 that I needed to make some changes. I didn't want to loathe my body any longer. I didn't want to be at war with myself for the second half of my life like I had been the first. Writing *Fat Girl* was the first step of my catharsis; next, I started to read and look for bopo inspiration, and then I found Instagram, and I was hooked.

But it's still work. It's not confidence or bravery. It's a choice I make to view my body with love and acceptance. To take a stand and say it's okay that I'm not thin and may never be again. I'm not going to put off anything I want to do because of my weight. I'm not going to spend the next several decades of my life miserable just because I don't look a certain way. I have enough problems with depression without hating my body too—to be perfectly honest.

I realized that others might think I just woke up like this one day and decided to be confident and show my body. They didn't see all the work I put into coming to terms with the messages I received as a child or the steps I took to eliminate the effects of diet culture on my outlook. They don't know how many thousands of beautiful plus-sized bodies I looked at, so many that those bodies began to look normal to me—so many that I realized *my* body was just like *theirs*, and yet different and unique all at the same time.

Maybe this will happen to you too—but the first time I saw a plus-sized model on Instagram who was roughly the same size and shape as me, I nearly cried. I was like, *wow, that is MY body!* And then I glanced at the comments, of the hundreds and thousands of people who were expressing their admiration for that plus-sized body. It was glorious!

So I tried to come up with all the steps, all the points of contemplation I could think of that would help someone get to the point I am finally at almost five years after writing *Fat Girl*. I condensed five years of work into one—so if it feels long, then remember that!

My journey is still not over. I still have bad days. I still have to make the choice. Some mornings I wake up, and my body hurts so bad from something I did the day before (gardening is usually a sure-fire culprit) I think, how the hell can I be this Bopo Goddess? I can't love my body today! I feel like a pile of dog doo.

But then I realize it's all part of the journey, and tomorrow I'll look in the mirror and think, "Hey, I'm rocking these leggings!"

So what's next for me on my journey? Well, my husband is the idealist in our relationship (I'm the realist, if you couldn't already tell), and he's always dreaming big about my books. Sometimes I think he has a lot more faith and confidence in me than I do. But he said, "What if this book really takes off and you become famous and are asked to speak all over the world? Would you be okay with that?"

It probably won't happen. I'm used to writing romance novels and then drowning in a huge sea of obscurity like a lot of other romance authors. But this book is different. It definitely brings something new to the table with the journaling component, so you never know.

I guess at this point, I'm just anxious to see what lies ahead. I know whatever happens, I'll never regret the honesty and rawness I put into this book. I won't regret sharing some of the personal battles I've fought. And I hope you won't regret buying it, either! I just hope I have created a platform where I can share what I've learned with other women, whether it's confined to this book and my social media accounts, or whether the opportunity arises to take this show on the road and reach women all over the world.

But wait, there's more! Your bopo journey doesn't stop here. The next part of the book is a series of daily reflections. Some of them are affirmations you can repeat to yourself, whereas some are questions to reflect on and journal. I hope now that you've gotten into the habit of journaling, you will continue, even after the 365 days are up. You never know, you might just want to write your own book when you're done!

Thank you so much for reading this and for helping me reaffirm my own commitment to loving my body, which I definitely did while I was writing. Now more than ever, as I approach the Big 5-0 and menopause and all the other wonderful aspects of aging, I need a body positive mindset to get me through. I hope you joined my Facebook group so we can continue to support each other. (https://www.facebook.com/groups/FGGLYB/ in case you didn't see it before.)

Now, you have more work to do… Your daily meditations begin on the next page.

Daily Bopo Meditations

The way I intend these to be used (but feel free to tell me to eff off and do your own thing) is to read and reflect on the statement or question, then write a little bit about one or more of the following:

- how you plan to love your body today
- negative thoughts you want to tell the fuck off
- vent about anyone in your life who has thwarted your body positive journey
- any self-care you plan to do
- a kind thing you plan to do for someone else today
- something you learned about yourself recently

You know, something along those lines. It's your journal, so those are just ideas. You do you, boo! The point is to be in the habit of being present and in the moment. Journals are great for that and taking stock of where you've been and where you're going. Journals are the best.

I'm not going to date the affirmations so you can start them on whatever day you want. You can fill that part in yourself. If you're doing this as an ebook instead of the paperback, you can write your journal entries in your notebook, on your blog, or wherever your little heart desires. The important thing is to write.

Here's something I want to make very clear: the reason I included 365 meditations is because learning to love your body is not an overnight process. It's not a two-week or two-month process either. After an entire year of focusing on changing your mindset and the way you view your body, however, you should start to see an improvement. These meditations are meant to keep your focus on all things body positive.

Now I don't want you coming to me after a few weeks and saying, "Krista, you promised me I'd learn to love my body. But I don't! You suck!"

Because I'm going to ask, "Did you finish all 365 of your bopo meditations?"

Then you're going to look at me sheepishly and shake your head.

And I'm going to say, "Do the entire year's worth of work, and then we'll talk."

Got it?

❀ Day 1
Date:

Remember when your mom used to say *It's what's on the inside that counts?*

That was just another thing she was right about.

❀ Day 2
Date:

My worth is not measured by the size of my waist.

Day 3
Date:

How can you move your body today in a way that will celebrate it? Don't just write about it…actually do it, too!

Day 4
Date:

Do you have pets? What do you think they think of your body?

Oh, that's right, they love you just the way you are!

Smart animals ☺

🌸 Day 5
Date:

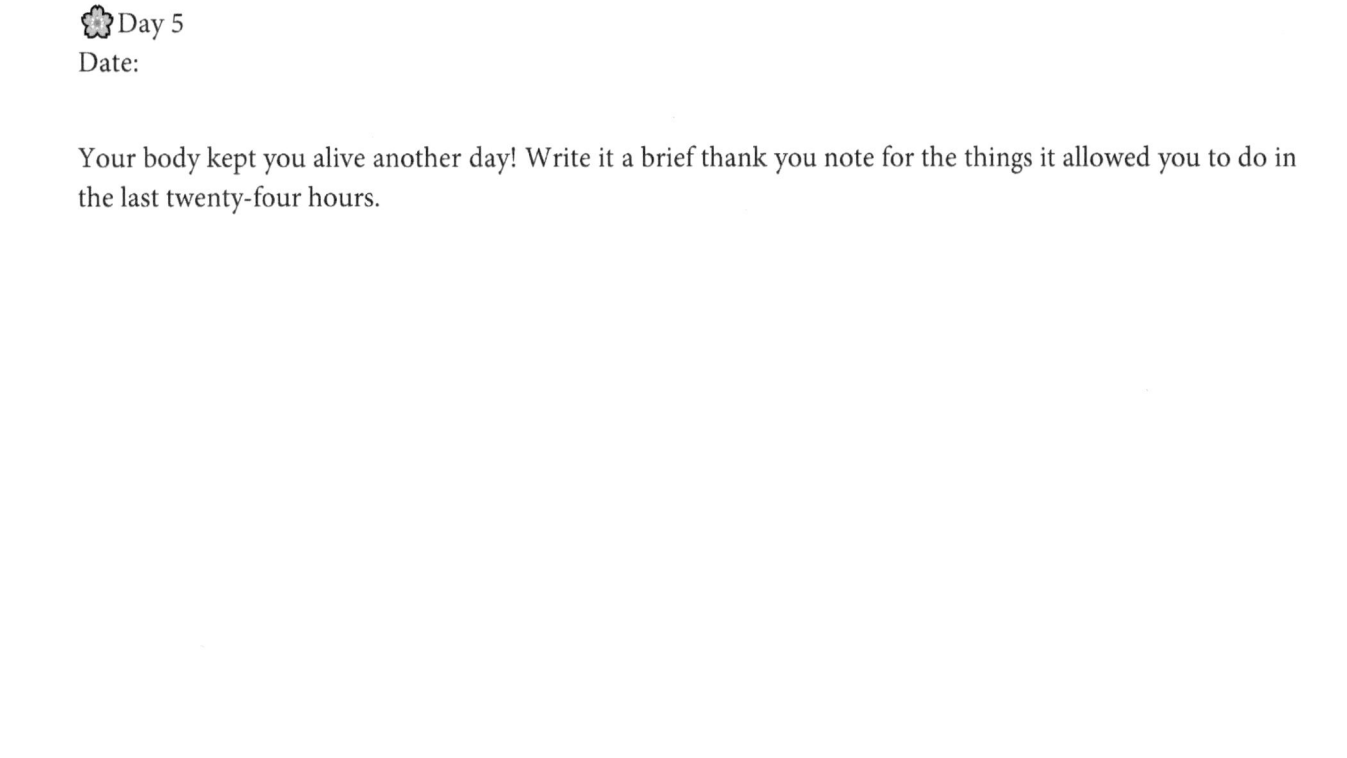

Your body kept you alive another day! Write it a brief thank you note for the things it allowed you to do in the last twenty-four hours.

🌸 Day 6
Date:

Think about the most beautiful and perfect woman you know. I guarantee you, absolutely 100% that she hates at least one part of her body and sometimes struggles with self-love sometimes too.

❀ Day 7
Date:

I was not put on this earth to be pretty or lose weight.

❀ Day 8
Date:
If you're a mom, and you've been pressured to "get your body back" after your child was born, well, screw those people. You never lost your body. It's been right here with you the whole time! And it gave you a beautiful baby!

✿ Day 9
Date:

Look at your hands. Think of five wonderful things about them and what they can do.

✿ Day 10
Date:

Think about a place where your body comes alive. If you can't go there today, think about planning a trip there soon.

❀ Day 11
Date:

Wear something that makes you feel amazing today. What did you choose?

❀ Day 12
Date:

There is only one ME in the entire universe. I am a precious gem. One of a kind.

✿ Day 13
Date:

My body needs and deserves food. Food is not my enemy.

✿ Day 14
Date:

I am allowed to take up space.

✿ Day 15
Date:

How I feel about my body is MY choice. I will not allow others to make that choice for me.

✿ Day 16
Date:

When others criticize my body, that's their problem, not mine.

🌸 Day 17
Date:

Body, I'm sorry for being cruel to you. I promise to love and cherish you always.

🌸 Day 18
Date:

How are you going to take care of your body today?

🌸 Day 19
Date:

A body part I felt ashamed of was _____. But these days I realize it's great because _____.

🌸 Day 20
Date:

Health has nothing to do with size.

🌸 Day 21
Date:

Today I will listen to myself and trust my inner judgment.

🌸 Day 22
Date:

Yesterday I promised to trust my inner judgment. I did that by _____.

🌸 Day 23
Date:

Eat something today that you really enjoy! What will it be?

🌸 Day 24
Date:

My body is merely a vessel for a whole lot of awesomeness.

🌸 Day 25
Date:

What have you put off doing because of your weight? Make a commitment to doing it today. What is it, and when will you do it?

🌸 Day 26
Date:

Food does not have a moral label. It is not good or bad. It's just food.

🌸 Day 27
Date:

Compliment at least three people today on something that does NOT involve looks.

🌸 Day 28
Date:

I deserve to be treated with love and respect.

🌸 Day 29
Date:

List three people you could call if you are in crisis.

🌸 Day 30
Date:

Who is someone you admire because of the way they love and accept themselves as is?

🌸 Day 31
Date:

My body can do awesome things! Here are a few of them:

🌸 Day 32
Date:

I'm not going to waste any more of my life wallowing in self-loathing or self-pity because of my size or weight.

🌸 Day 33
Date:

Accepting myself as I am is the first step in evolving into the person I want to be.

🌸 Day 34
Date:

Photos in magazines and advertisements are all airbrushed and photoshopped.

🌸 Day 35
Date:

My age does not define me. I refuse to accept that I'm "too old" for anything.

🌸 Day 36
Date:

I make the world a better place by being in it. Here's how:

❁ Day 37
Date:

My opinion of myself is the only one that counts.

❁ Day 38
Date:

My identity is based on who I am on the inside, not the outside.

❀ Day 39
Date:

I deserve love, respect, and happiness.

❀ Day 40
Date:

No food has any power over me. It's just food.

🌸 Day 41
Date:

My life is happening now. It doesn't start when I lose X pounds or wear X size. I'm going to live it now!

🌸 Day 42
Date:

List one way you plan to take care of yourself today:

🌸 Day 43
Date:

Today I'm going to move my body by _____.

🌸 Day 44
Date:

One thing I love about myself is _____.

❀ Day 45
Date:

If your friend asked you to go on a diet with her, what would you say?

❀ Day 46
Date:

List something about yourself you're really proud of.

❀ Day 47
Date:

Beauty is in the eye of the beholder. You're the beholder of YOU.

❀ Day 48
Date:

You deserve to wear clothes that make you feel good about yourself.

🌸 Day 49
Date:

I have a purpose in life.

🌸 Day 50
Date:

You made it through 50 of these! You should buy yourself something nice or do something nice for yourself! You deserve a treat 😊

❀ Day 51
Date:

I'm a superhero because _____.

❀ Day 52
Date:

I am perfect just the way I am.

❀ Day 53
Date:

Beauty has no size.

❀ Day 54
Date:

I choose to do and say kind things for and about myself.

❀ Day 55
Date:

The body you have now is the only body you will ever get. The life you have now is the only life you will ever get. So enjoy them both!

❀ Day 56
Date:

You can have fitness goals or health goals that don't involve weighing yourself or losing weight. List one or two of yours:

Day 57
Date:

People who tear other people down are sad, lonely, little people. Be a person who builds people up!

Day 58
Date:

What is one thing you'd like to go back and tell your sixteen-year-old self?

❀ Day 59
Date:

Name one thing you're going to do for yourself today.

❀ Day 60
Date:

I deserve good things in my life. I deserve to be happy.

❀ Day 61
Date:

I'm not responsible for other people's feelings or actions.

❀ Day 62
Date:

I will wear whatever the hell I want to wear, regardless of my age or weight, thank you very much.

✿ Day 63
Date:

I will tell people who say they are concerned about my health when they disparage my weight to mind their own (fucking) business. *Okay, you can leave out the F bomb if you want, but when I say it, I'm leaving it in!*

✿ Day 64
Date:

I cannot control others. I can only control myself.

🌸 Day 65
Date:

Name something physical you can do today to celebrate how your body moves.

🌸 Day 66
Date:

Try to spend some time in nature today. Don't forget you're a part of nature too.

❀ Day 67
Date:

I will not apologize for my thoughts, opinions, ideas, or for taking up space.

❀ Day 68
Date:

Plan a fun trip with your friends or significant other. Where will you go? Now actually plan it. I mean it!

❀ Day 69
Date:

When was the last time you felt sexy? What would you need to do today to get that feeling back? (Hey, it's Day 69. I couldn't help myself!)

❀ Day 70
Date:

You are the author of your own life story. So make it a good one! (This is hanging on my office wall above the bookcase that holds all the books I've written!)

❀ Day 71
Date:

Listen to one of the songs on the Inspirational AF playlist (at the beginning of the book). How does it make you feel?

❀ Day 72
Date:

You are enough. Just the way you are.

🌸 Day 73
Date:

Everyone struggles to love their body. EVERYONE. What you might consider someone's best feature might be one they loathe. What you might consider your worst feature might be the one others love about you.

🌸 Day 74
Date:

Diversity is beautiful! The world would be boring and ugly if we all looked the same.

❀ Day 75:
Date:

Find a body positive Instagram account to follow and comment on one of their posts.

❀ Day 76
Date:

You are the CEO of your life. You decide who to hire, fire and promote!

🌸 Day 77
Date:

Your body hair is NOT unnatural or gross.

🌸 Day 78
Date:

Wrinkles, cellulite and stretch marks are completely normal.

❀ Day 79
Date:

I'm making a conscious choice to love my body today.

❀ Day 80
Date:

Diet Culture is a real thing, and it's a destructive force that needs to be stopped.

🌸 Day 81
Date:

Age is only a number. My age does not define me.

🌸 Day 82
Date:

The only "diet" I'm concerned about is the diet of images and messages I hear from the media, entertainment, social media, advertising, and people in my life.

🌸 Day 83
Date:

I'm going to be a body positive role model to someone else today. Here's how:

🌸 Day 84
Date:

Reach out to a friend you haven't heard from in a while and ask if she's okay.

❀ Day 85
Date:

I won't be afraid to express my opinions today. My opinions are as valid as anyone else's.

❀ Day 86
Date:

My body shape does not make me any more or less feminine.

🌸 Day 87
Date:

It's okay to cut toxic people out of your life.

🌸 Day 88
Date:

If I exercise, it's because it's good for my body and mind, not because it's a chore, or I need to lose weight, or I have to work off that piece of cheesecake I ate.

❀ Day 89
Date:

If you don't like where you are, move. You are not a tree.

❀ Day 90
Date:

Change is not a bad word. Change is an opportunity for growth.

❀ Day 91
Date:

Food doesn't control me. I control food.

❀ Day 92
Date:

You can't tell someone's health by looking at them.

Day 93
Date:

I will not judge people by their appearance. I will not make assumptions about people based on their size, what they're wearing, their hairstyles, or any other physical attributes. People all deserve a basic level of human decency and respect.

Day 94
Date:

I won't let my kids hear me say negative comments about my weight or size OR anyone else's weight or size.

🌸 Day 95
Date:

People of all genders, sizes, shapes, ages, abilities, colors, backgrounds, and faiths matter and are equal.

🌸 Day 96
Date:

I don't have to take other people's advice. My own intuition and decision-making ability are pretty damn awesome.

🌸 Day 97
Date:

When was the last time you enjoyed your favorite treat? Today is a good day! (What did you choose?)

🌸 Day 98
Date:

If you're a mom and you're feeling bad about your stretch marks or bigger body after giving birth, go look at that beautiful life you created and remind yourself that you are amazing.

❀ Day 99
Date:

Authenticity is better than beauty ANY DAY.

❀ Day 100
Date:

You made it to day 100! Congratulations! How has your self-image changed in the past 100 days?

Day 101
Date:

Fat is not a bad word. If you use it to describe yourself and someone tries to correct you, tell them you have reclaimed it, and you would appreciate it if they didn't try to take it away from you.

IT IS OKAY TO BE FAT!

Day 102
Date:

Call out fatphobia when you see it. It's so deeply ingrained in our way of thinking, many people don't even realize when they're being fatphobic.

❀ Day 103
Date:

If you've been bullied about your weight, you are allowed to be upset and angry about it. You did NOT deserve to be treated that way, and you deserve healing and happiness.

❀ Day 104
Date:

Next time you go to the doctor, if they harass you about your BMI, tell them to stick their BMI chart where the sun don't shine.

(Haha, okay so maybe don't really say that. But you could cite some studies about how inaccurate BMI charts are and how they are inherently racist and sexist.

https://www.npr.org/templates/story/story.php?storyId=106268439)

❀ Day 105
Date:

Try to wear some color today! You can wear whatever colors, patterns, or prints you want!

❀ Day 106
Date:

You are not on this earth to be pretty or thin. You are here for a much higher purpose!

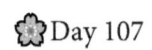

❀ Day 107
Date:
Weight fluctuations in either direction are completely normal and don't need to be commented about publicly, nor do they have anything to do with how good of a person you are.

❀ Day 108
Date:

If you have given birth, you lost the baby weight when the baby was born. The baby was the baby weight. End of story.

❀ Day 109
Date:

Diet culture doesn't want to make you thin. It only wants to make itself richer.

❀ Day 110
Date:

My life wouldn't be easier or better if I were thin. My life would be easier and better if our culture wasn't obsessed with thinness.

❀Day 111
Date:

My stomach isn't there to be flat or have sexy abs. It's there to contain organs so I can digest food and live and stuff.

❀Day 112
Date:

You can enjoy sex no matter what your size. You deserve to feel good, sexy, loved, and desired.

❀ Day 113
Date:

Your body doesn't care why you might want to lose weight. All it knows is it's not supposed to be treated like that unless something is very wrong.

❀ Day 114
Date:

Give yourself permission to enjoy something today whether it's a certain type of food, some form of entertainment, or retail therapy. Feel no guilt!

🌸 Day 115
Date:

Hey, newsflash, thin people get diabetes, heart disease and other medical problems too. And they are more likely to get better healthcare than fat people when they do.

🌸 Day 116
Date:

Try to find one good thing about every person you deal with today, even the nastiest person. Fill your heart and mind with love and positivity.

✿ Day 117
Date:

Losing weight is not a miracle cure for ANYTHING.

✿ Day 118
Date:

Thoughts and words have power. Here's how these daily doses of #bopo are helping me:

❀ Day 119
Date:

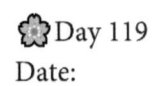

I love and accept myself unconditionally.

❀ Day 120
Date:

Food is not my enemy. It keeps me alive!

🌸 Day 121
Date:

A friend who helps me on my bopo journey is _____. She helps me by _____.

🌸 Day 122
Date:

Tell your family how they can help you on your bopo journey.

❀ Day 123
Date:

My needs are just as important as everyone else's needs.

❀ Day 124
Date:

My flaws make me unique, and I refuse to disparage myself because of them.

✿ Day 125
Date:

You're not fat. You HAVE fat. You also have fingernails, but you're not fingernails. (That would be super weird, right?) *Just a note: I actually don't mind using fat as a descriptor, but I did think this was funny and insightful.*

✿ Day 126
Date:

I will not let my mind bully my body!

🌸 Day 127
Date:

My body loves me! Look how hard it works to keep me alive!

🌸 Day 128
Date:

My body will take on many shapes in my lifetime. It is my character that is MOST important.

Day 129
Date:

Judging someone by their appearance doesn't define THEM. It defines YOU.

Day 130
Date:

You're most beautiful when you're YOURSELF, not when you try to be someone else.

🌸 Day 131
Date:

I move my body because I love it, not because I hate it.

🌸 Day 132
Date:

The scale only tells you the numerical value of your gravitational pull. It doesn't tell you your value.

❀ Day 133
Date:

I will not compare myself to strangers on the internet or social media.

❀ Day 134
Date:

What people choose to show of themselves on social media is not the truth.

❁ Day 135
Date:

Body confidence doesn't come from trying to achieve the perfect body. It comes from embracing the one you already have.

❁ Day 136
Date:

When was the last time you had a YOU day? Where you did what YOU wanted to do ALL DAY? Plan one of those soon!

❀ Day 137
Date:

Loving your body only when it's in perfect shape is like loving your kids only when they're well-behaved.

❀ Day 138
Date:

You are a force of nature! (Use your power for good!)

🌸 Day 139
Date:

Not coming along as fast as you'd like with this bopo stuff? Be patient! How many years were you bombarded with negative messages? It's going to take more than 139 days to undo some of that shit!

🌸 Day 140
Date:

Instead of obsessing over parts of your body you hate, obsess over the ones you love.

🌸 Day 141
Date:

How to have a bikini body: Have a body. Put on a bikini. That's it!

🌸 Day 142
Date:

The people in your life who really matter will love you no matter what size you are.

❀ Day 143
Date:

Your body hears everything your mind says.

❀ Day 144
Date:

There is no wrong way to have a body.

🌸 Day 145
Date:

Hating your body won't make you thin, and being thin won't make you stop hating your body.

🌸 Day 146
Date:

Your body is an INSTRUMENT, not an ORNAMENT. -Ariane Machin (Holy crap, I just saw that on a meme and I FLOVE it!)

❀ Day 147
Date:

If tomorrow, women woke up and decided they really liked their bodies, just think how many industries would go out of business. -Dr. Gail Dines

❀ Day 148
Date:

What is something you've never worn before because of your weight/size/shape/age? Challenge yourself to try it!

❀ Day 149
Date:

When was the last time you went without makeup? Try it today (or someday soon).

❀ Day 150
Date:

Congratulations, you made it to day 150! You deserve a treat. What will it be?

🌸 Day 151
Date:

Your body has been waiting your whole life for you to make peace with it.

🌸 Day 152
Date:

Today is an opportunity to love your body more than you did yesterday. How will you do that?

🌸 Day 153
Date:

Sexy is not a size. Every calorie is not a war. Your body is not a battleground. Your worth is not measured in pounds. You are just as worthy as any other woman.

🌸 Day 154
Date:

Your haters want you to be miserable. Think about how pissed off they'll be when you're happy and living your best life!

🌸 Day 155
Date:

You were born to be real—not perfect.

🌸 Day 156
Date:

Taking care of myself is not selfish.

❁ Day 157
Date:

Hating my body will never get me as far as loving it.

❁ Day 158
Date:

Your body is a tiny, trivial thing about you. So much more important are your dreams and aspirations, your mind, heart, and soul.

❀ Day 159
Date:

You don't need anyone else to say you're beautiful for you to be, in fact, beautiful. You don't need validation from anyone. (I'm tempted to put this one in twice because I need to hear it!)

❀ Day 160
Date:

Be the voice you needed to hear when you were younger.

❀ Day 161
Date:

The best thing you can wear is a smile and self-confidence.

❀ Day 162
Date:

How did your body take care of you today? Make sure to tell it thank you!

❀ Day 163
Date:

There's no such thing as clean eating or dirty eating. There's only eating.

❀ Day 164
Date:

No matter what my body looks like, it's what my heart looks like that matters most.

❀ Day 165
Date:

This body has overcome lots of obstacles and has the scars to prove it!

❀ Day 166
Date:

Today I will _____ to celebrate my body.

❀ Day 167
Date:

I will be a good example for the young girls in my life when it comes to how I talk about my body and others' bodies in front of them.

❀ Day 168
Date:

Today I'm really craving _____. And I'm going to satisfy that craving by _____.

🌸 Day 169
Date:

Here are just a few of the ways I'm strong:

🌸 Day 170
Date:

I am perfect, whole, and complete just the way I am.

🌸 Day 171
Date:

Today I'm going to block out any negative messages about my body, whether they come from me or someone else.

🌸 Day 172
Date:

I am brave enough to try something new. Here's my plan for trying _____.

Day 173
Date:

I'm going to take care of myself so I can be around for those I love.

Day 174
Date:

I am comfortable and confident in my own skin.

❀ Day 175
Date:

This body houses a goddess.

❀ Day 176
Date:

I will listen to my body with respect to when, what, and how much I should eat.

🌸 Day 177
Date:

My body allows me to experience the world around me.

🌸 Day 178
Date:

I will not regret growing older. Many do not get the privilege of growing old.

❀ Day 179
Date:

My body belongs to no one else but me.

❀ Day 180
Date:

I will practice self-care today by _____.

❀ Day 181
Date:

I am allowed to feel a full range of emotions. My emotions are valid, no matter what they are.

❀ Day 182
Date:

My body is a testament to the life I have lived.

🌸 Day 183
Date:

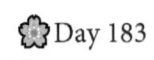

When someone treats me unfairly, I will remember that I can only control my reaction to it. I cannot control other people.

🌸 Day 184
Date:

A "goal weight" is an arbitrary number and doesn't define me or my success.

❀ Day 185
Date:

I won't compare myself to anyone else today.

❀ Day 186
Date:

Today I'm going to wear _____ because it makes me feel good.

🌸 Day 187
Date:

The only alternative to aging is death.

🌸 Day 188
Date:

It's my job to take care of me. I don't expect anyone else to do it, and it's not my job to take care of other healthy adults, either.

🌸 Day 189
Date:

Today I'm going to move my body by _____.

🌸 Day 190
Date:

I deserve happiness and love no matter what I eat or what I weigh.

❀ Day 191
Date:

My existence makes the world a better place.

❀ Day 192
Date:

I won't let my family tell me how to feel about myself.

🌸 Day 193
Date:

Restricting my food intake does not make me good, saintly, or virtuous.

🌸 Day 194
Date:

Binging doesn't make me bad or evil.

✿ Day 195
Date:

Life doesn't start when I lose X pounds. Life is happening RIGHT NOW.

✿ Day 196
Date:

Today, I'm going to enjoy and celebrate nature by _____.

🌸 Day 197
Date:

Being skinny doesn't make someone good. Being fat doesn't make someone bad. People's actions and the way they treat others determine if they are bad or good.

🌸 Day 198
Date:

I hold all the power to make my life amazing.

✿ Day 199
Date:

I'm going to share a body positive affirmation today with someone else.

✿ Day 200
Date:

Congratulations on making it to Day 200! I'm going to celebrate making it this far in my bopo journey by _____.

🌸 Day 201
Date:

Not everyone has to like me. As long as I like myself and treat others well, that's what really counts.

🌸 Day 202
Date:

My weight is the absolute least interesting thing about me.

❁ Day 203
Date:

My brain will have room for positive things when I let go of my obsession with my weight and body size.

❁ Day 204
Date:

Food is what keeps me alive. I refuse to feel bad about eating. I was made to eat.

❀ Day 205
Date:

This body is power. This body is strength. This body is love.

❀ Day 206
Date:

Growing wise is so much more important than shrinking my body.

❀ Day 207
Date:

I am a human, and I have flaws. We all do.

❀ Day 208
Date:

I will admit when I'm wrong, but I won't apologize for having feelings or being who I am.

🌸 Day 209
Date:

I'm going to try a new food this week. I choose _____.

🌸 Day 210
Date:

I've let my feelings about my body keep me from _____. I'm going to make a plan to _____ now that I feel better about my body.

🌸 Day 211
Date:

My skin protects me, and I'm going to protect it in return.

🌸 Day 212
Date:

I will surround myself with loving and supportive people. I will get rid of toxic people in my life.

❀ Day 213
Date:

Take a break from social media today or someday soon.

❀ Day 214
Date:

Today I'm the best version of myself that has ever lived.

❀ Day 215
Date:

I'm in control of my food choices.

❀ Day 216
Date:

I work hard, and I deserve to take time off to renew and recharge.

🌸 Day 217
Date:

I won't forget to take care of myself when I'm taking care of others.

🌸 Day 218
Date:

Loving myself is the greatest revolution.

🌸 Day 219
Date:

Like Eleanor Roosevelt said, "No one can make you feel inferior without your consent." She was a smart lady!

🌸 Day 220
Date:

Beauty comes in all shapes, sizes, and colors.

❀ Day 221
Date:

When I look in the mirror today, I'm only going to think positive things about what I see.

❀ Day 222
Date:

Plan a girls' night out, even if it's just dinner with one girlfriend. Record your plan here:

❀ Day 223
Date:

Take a break this week from worrying about body hair.

❀ Day 224
Date:

Think about a time that you felt you looked really good. What made you feel that way?

❀ Day 225
Date:

Name a body part that you're learning to accept. List all the positive things about it.

❀ Day 226
Date:

When was the last time you tried something new as far as your hair, makeup or skincare routine goes? Make a goal to change something up soon.

❀ Day 227
Date:

Today, find five minutes and just empty your mind of everything but your breathing. Just *be* for five minutes.

❀ Day 228
Date:

I will think a kind thought about every person I see today.

🌸 Day 229
Date:

If there's a holiday or social event coming up, think about how you will manage it, whether it's by committing to eating whatever you want or by avoiding toxic people who will sap your joy. Prepare yourself and have a plan for making it as enjoyable as possible.

🌸 Day 230
Date:

Try to catch either the sunrise or sunset today.

❀ Day 231
Date:

I'm worthy of love and respect because I am a human. My weight, size, and age have nothing to do with my worthiness.

❀ Day 232
Date:

Do you have a pet? Try to spend some time around a pet or animals today. Spending time with pets has been proven to have a positive effect on people's moods and well-being.

❁ Day 233
Date:

I will be a good example of body positivity to the younger generation by_____.

❁ Day 234
Date:

Thin people don't always love their bodies. Having a negative body image isn't something reserved solely for people of size.

✿ Day 235
Date:

Expose yourself to some bopo media/entertainment today. Listen to a bopo song, read a bopo book (I can make recommendations!), or follow a bopo social media account.

✿ Day 236
Date:

Think about a happy memory from your childhood today.

🌸 Day 237
Date:

Today I will practice self-care by _____.

🌸 Day 238
Date:

When was the last time you had a really good laugh?

❀ Day 239
Date:

If you've been putting off making an appointment for your health (physical or mental), DO IT TODAY!

❀ Day 240
Date:

My body is a gift, and I cherish all the amazing things it can do.

🌸 Day 241
Date:

Here is a short list of some of the things my body can do:

🌸 Day 242
Date:

My body and mind work in tandem—and make a pretty good team!

❀ Day 243
Date:

The most beautiful thing about my mind is_____.

❀ Day 244
Date:

I forgive myself for _____.

Day 245
Date:

A healthy choice I'm going to make today is _____.

 Day 246
Date:

Other women are not my competition. We are all on the same team!

❀ Day 247
Date:

My body is a temple to decorate as I please. Today I'll do that by _____.

❀ Day 248
Date:

An obstacle I've overcome recently is _____.

🌸 Day 249
Date:

Today I'm going to listen to my body so it can get the food, rest, and activity it needs.

🌸 Day 250
Date:

I've made it through 250 daily affirmations, and I'm still struggling with _____. Here's my plan for making it easier:

🌸 Day 251
Date:

My inner wisdom will guide my choices today and always.

🌸 Day 252
Date:

Growing older is a blessing. Here is one thing I've learned in the last decade of my life that I didn't know in the previous decade: _____.

❀ Day 253
Date:

A flower does not think of competing with the flower next to it. It just blooms.

❀ Day 254
Date:

Today I'm going to unfollow accounts on social media that make me feel bad about my body.

❀ Day 255
Date:

Cellulite is normal and having it does not detract from my beauty or worth.

❀ Day 256
Date:

There is no right or wrong way to be a woman, just different ways.

❀ Day 257
Date:

Life is too short to spend it at war with myself.

❀ Day 258
Date:

I will wear whatever style of clothing that makes me feel empowered and good about myself. I won't judge others' fashion choices.

❀ Day 259
Date:

Never apologize for being confident. If you're going to be passionate about something, doesn't it make sense to be about YOU?

❀ Day 260
Date:

Beware of people who drain your energy or leave you feeling negative, and do your best to avoid contact with those people.

Day 261
Date:

You can be fat and beautiful. The two are not mutually exclusive.

Day 262
Date:

Foods are not good or evil. They're just food. Repeat it over and over until you believe it.

❀ Day 263
Date:

Stretch marks are completely normal.

❀ Day 264
Date:

What's wrong with a muffin top? Muffins are delicious. Mmmmmmm.

🌸 Day 265
Date:

One hundred days to go!!! Reach out to a friend today to see how she's doing.

🌸 Day 266
Date:

Guess what's more important than what size jeans you wear? Literally EVERYTHING else!

🌸 Day 267
Date:

Next time you hear "Men prefer…" eradicate that phrase from your brain. Who cares what men prefer? Do what YOU prefer.

🌸 Day 268
Date:

You're not perfect, and that's okay. Guess what?! No one else is either.

🌸 Day 269
Date:

Beauty standards are made up and change from decade to decade and generation to generation.

🌸 Day 270
Date:

You're defined by who you are and how you treat others, not by what you look like.

❀ Day 271
Date:

If your thighs touch, you're one step closer to being a mermaid, so who's the real winner here? (hehe!)

❀ Day 272
Date:

The last time I had a really good cry over something was _____.

🌸 Day 273
Date:

I won't let anyone dismiss or invalidate my feelings today.

🌸 Day 274
Date:

Don't unscrew another woman's lightbulb in order for you to shine more brightly.

❀ Day 275
Date:

Today I'm going to move my body by _____.

❀ Day 276
Date:

Losing weight only makes you lighter. It does not make you kinder, smarter, more creative, more passionate, more determined or happier.

❀ Day 277
Date:

Being negative about your body won't make it thinner.

❀ Day 278
Date:

When was the last time you did something nice for yourself? Plan to do something soon!

❀ Day 279
Date:

Ladies, you don't need validation from men. Validate yourself.

❀ Day 280
Date:

The most important thing you can be is kind—to yourself and others.

🌸 Day 281
Date:

Here's a new detox diet for you: cleanse yourself of all toxic body ideals and eat whatever you want. You'll feel super duper refreshed!

🌸 Day 282
Date:

My body might not be perfect, but it does a great job holding all my organs in place!

🌸 Day 283
Date:

If you have children of your own or are around children, think about how you can be a bopo influence for them. List some ways here:

🌸 Day 284
Date:

You don't owe anyone a flat stomach or thin thighs.

🌸 Day 285
Date:

Don't just let go of toxic things like diet culture and body shaming—let go of toxic people too.

🌸 Day 286
Date:

Embrace your body—it is the most important and valuable thing you will ever own.

❀ Day 287
Date:

You will never ever ever please everyone.

❀ Day 288
Date:

A quote from my book *Given to Fly* – "I may be fat, but at least I'm not fake!"

🌸 Day 289
Date:

Don't apologize for being who you are.

🌸 Day 290
Date:

You don't owe it to anyone to try to make yourself smaller.

❀ Day 291
Date:

If I have a health issue, I'm going to seek out a doctor who treats me with respect.

❀ Day 292
Date:

I will wear clothes I'm comfortable in and make me feel good about myself, regardless of any fashion rules.

❀ Day 293
Date:

I will treat other people the way I want to be treated.

❀ Day 294
Date:

I refuse to dwell in the past. It cannot be changed. The only way to go is forward.

🌸 Day 295
Date:

I don't need to put anyone down to feel better about myself.

🌸 Day 296
Date:

One area of my life in which I'm working toward having better balance is _____.

❀ Day 297
Date:

I won't try to be anyone else but myself.

❀ Day 298
Date:

Loving my body is not a linear process; it's more of a meandering path. It's a marathon, not a sprint. I'm fine with taking the long, scenic route.

❀ Day 299
Date:

Moving my body isn't punishment; it's a celebration. Here's how I moved my body today:

This next series of #bopo meditations come from my readers.

❀ Day 300
Date:

She believed she could, so she did. – contributed by Kelli Harper

Day 301
Date:

Sometimes the road you travel doesn't lead to the destination you hoped for. But you can look back on the trip and still smile—then it was worth it. – contributed by Theresa Polifka Jakab

Day 302
Date:

It's a good day for a good day! – contributed by Jennifer Rose Newell

❀ Day 303
Date:

I am strong and capable, and worthy of love. – contributed by Tamara Sherill Lang

❀ Day 304
Date:

Life's too short to be unkind to yourself. – contributed by Colleen Quirk

❀ Day 305
Date:

There is good to be done in this world that can only be done by thinking like a girl, acting like a girl, and fighting like a girl. – contributed by Jennie Lee Ersari

❀ Day 306
Date:

I am not responsible for other people's reactions to my actions. – contributed by Rebecca Moninghoff

❀ Day 307
Date:

Happiness looks different for everyone. – contributed by Linda Landers

❀ Day 308
Date:

I'm not scared to be seen. I make no apologies. This is me! – contributed by Kayleigh Woods

✿ Day 309
Date:

Self-love is not selfish; it is essential. – contributed by T.L. Clark

✿ Day 310
Date:

Believe in yourself, and you will be unstoppable. – contributed by Jo-Ann Toth

🌸 Day 311
Date:

Today I will give thanks to the millions of wonderful things my body does just to keep me alive. – contributed by T.L. Clark

🌸 Day 312
Date:

Don't wait until you've reached your goal to be proud of yourself. Be proud of every step you take toward reaching your goal. – contributed by Theresa Polifka Jakab

Day 313
Date:

You are amazing. Own that shit. – contributed by Colleen Quirk

Day 314
Date:

Things you CAN'T recover in life:

1. the stone after it's thrown
2. the word after it's said
3. the occasion after it's missed
4. the time after it's gone

-contributed by Theresa Polifka Jakab

❀ Day 315
Date:

My body is a symbol of my life journey. – contributed by T.L. Clark

❀ Day 316
Date:

Your weight will fluctuate; your value will not. – contributed by Colleen Quirk

❁ Day 317
Date:

If I could see myself through my daughter's eyes, I'd know my true worth and strength. – contributed by Sarah Coulson

❁ Day 318
Date:

I've earned every scar, scrape, and blemish; they are what make me *me*. They are beautiful in His sight, and I won't be ashamed of them. – contributed by Charlene McDonnough

🌸 Day 319
Date:

Every day is a blank page for you to write your story. – contributed by Sarah Nolan

🌸 Day 320
Date:

The last time I felt really good about myself was _____.

🌸 Day 321
Date:

The sexiest part of my body is my brain.

🌸 Day 322
Date:

Today, I'll enjoy nature by _____.

❀ Day 323
Date:

Just another reminder that every photo you see in advertisements is airbrushed and/or photoshopped.

❀ Day 324
Date:

Never forget that diet culture doesn't care about you or your health. All they care about is making money off your insecurities and feelings of inferiority. DON'T LET THEM PROFIT OFF YOU.

🌸 Day 325
Date:

A reminder that carbs are not evil!

🌸 Day 326
Date:

When was the last time you treated yourself? It's time, don't you think?

🌸 Day 327
Date:

I am in charge of how I feel today, and today I'm choosing happiness.

🌸 Day 328
Date:

Remember the 4 Happy P's? (Places, People, Passions & Pleasures). Choose a Happy P to experience this week. What will it be?

🌸 Day 329
Date:

Our standards of beauty and size are distorted by the media.

🌸 Day 330
Date:

I won't make assumptions about people based on their looks.

❀ Day 331
Date:

My body, my rules. Society can fuck off!

❀ Day 332
Date:

I don't need to change for anyone but myself—and only if I choose to.

❀ Day 333
Date:

This body is just the keeper of my magic. Who cares where it folds or dimples?

❀ Day 334
Date:

What would happen if one day all women woke up and decided enough is enough and decided to love themselves just the way they are?

❀ Day 335
Date:

I'm going to try something new this week—a new food, a new place to visit, a new activity. Here's what it'll be:

❀ Day 336
Date:

If I have a day where I'm body-shaming myself, I'm going to go on Instagram and search the hashtag #bodypositive.

🌸 Day 337
Date:

Haterz gonna hate. And I'm not a hater.

🌸 Day 338
Date:

I'm worth fighting for.

❀ Day 339
Date:

"The minute you learn to love yourself, you will not want to be anybody else." – Rihanna

❀ Day 340
Date:

Body positivity isn't just for women. Men have body image issues too, and I won't hold them to different or unrealistic standards.

🌸 Day 341
Date:

Moving my body creates endorphins, and those make me feel amazing! I'm going to make some endorphins by _____ today.

🌸 Day 342
Date:

My motivation comes from within, not from others.

❀ Day 343
Date:

Whether I have large, small, sagging, or scarred breasts, I'm still as much of a woman as any other.

❀ Day 344
Date:

When I look in the mirror, I will look at my body as a whole and not scrutinize and criticize individual parts. I'm a whole person.

🌸 Day 345
Date:

I am strong enough to remove toxic and body-shaming people from my life. I deserve respect no matter my size or shape.

🌸 Day 346
Date:

How have you been a good example for body positivity this week?

🌸 Day 347
Date:

Life is too short to keep telling yourself you'll do X when you lose weight. Life is happening now.

🌸 Day 348
Date:

You deserve love. You deserve to be happy.

🌸 Day 349
Date:

The only thing standing in the way between you and happiness is YOU.

🌸 Day 350
Date:

I'm going to get a good night's sleep tonight. I deserve to rest!

✿ Day 351
Date:

I'm taking care of myself today by _____.

✿ Day 352
Date:

Call a friend and check up on her today.

🌸 Day 353
Date:

A woman's job is not to be pretty or to be attractive to men.

🌸 Day 354
Date:

What's your plan of action when feelings of inadequacy and self-loathing creep in? Write that shit down!

❀ Day 355
Date:

I won't compare myself to others.

❀ Day 356
Date:

There is no such thing as a perfect person, body, or relationship.

🌸 Day 357
Date:

Take a selfie today. If you took a selfie when you first started this process, compare them. Is it easier to look at yourself now in pictures?

🌸 Day 358
Date:

A food I've always avoided because it's "bad" for me is _____. I give myself permission to eat as much of it as I want.

❀ Day 359
Date:

A fun way to move my body is _____.

❀ Day 360
Date:

Loving my body is a journey and a choice. It's going to take a while, and I have to actively choose to do it.

🌸 Day 361
Date:

Here's what I've learned about myself after almost a year of daily meditations:

🌸 Day 362
Date:

I can spread the word about body positivity by:

❀ Day 363
Date:

I trust myself around food. Food is not the enemy, not a weapon, not a punishment, and not a reward. It's a fuel.

❀ Day 364
Date:

Listen to a song on the bopo playlist today. How did it make you feel?

❁ Day 365
Date:

Congratulations, you did it!!! How will you continue to empower yourself to love your body now that this book is complete?

YOU DID IT!

Here's a certificate you can fill out and post somewhere you'll see it to remind yourself of your commitment to loving your body. https://mountainswanted.com/wp-content/uploads/Fat-Girl-Completion-Certificate.pdf

You put in a lot of work this past year, and I hope you've come out the other side with a greater love and deeper appreciation for your body from the top of your head to your pinky toe, as well as for your mind, heart, and soul.

Thanks again for going on a bopo journey with me, and all the best to you!

If you've enjoyed this book, please leave a review on the retailer of your choice, or Goodreads or BookBub. And if you want to check out my other books or join my newsletter, head on over to www.klmontgomery.com and put your email address in the pop-up!

Acknowledgments

First off, I need to thank my husband, who, even though he has a long way to go in his own body positive journey, always supports mine and all my crazy ideas for books. And he even read the first couple chapters of this one and told me not to sell myself short when I listed all of my shortcomings as far as qualifications to write this book are concerned. He's been with me every step of my journey from writing *Fat Girl* to now, so he knows how much I have grown.

Secondly, I want to thank the ladies who are part of the Facebook group I created to accompany this book. The fact that you believe in me and support me means the absolute world to me. I know you'll also, as founding members of the group, be instrumental in building the body positive community I envision in that space. A special thank you to those who contributed Bopo Meditations for the end of the book!

Thirdly, I must thank my dear friend Colleen Noyes of Itsy Bitsy Book Bits. She's always been my biggest supporter in the book industry, and I'm so thrilled that we've grown closer as friends as well. I definitely consider you a part of my tribe, beautiful lady!

Next, a huge thank you to my proofreader Tina Kissinger and my personal assistant, Jared Gallant. You guys make my life SO MUCH EASIER!

Finally, a huge thank you to the bopo Instagrammers I follow who have made such a huge difference in my life and my mindset. I don't know where I'd be right now if it weren't for you. Thank you for sharing yourselves with the world.

About the Author

K.L. Montgomery writes #bodypositive sweet romance and romcom. A librarian in a former life, she now works as an editor and runs the nearly 5000-member Indie Author Support group on Facebook, in addition to publishing romance novels under two names.

Though she remains a Hoosier at heart, K.L. shares her coastal Delaware home with some furry creatures and her husband, who works in law enforcement. She has an undying love for her three sons, Broadway musicals, the beach, Seinfeld, the color teal, IU basketball, paisleys, and dark chocolate.

Visit K.L.'s website at http://www.klmontgomery.com and sign up for her newsletter. You can follow her on Facebook at http://www.facebook.com/GreenCastles, Twitter (@KLMontgomery8) or Instagram (k.l.montgomery)

Also By K.L. Montgomery

Contemporary Romance

Given to Fly

From the author of *Fat Girl* comes this sweet bodypositive romance with a single dad hero and a heroine faced with a life-changing choice.

Annelise Lowe was taught that if she was a good enough person and Christian, all life's puzzle pieces would simply fall into place. God would bless her with a happy marriage and children of her own. But those promises were shattered when she came face to face with her husband's infidelity and her own infertility.

The one unbiased friend she can lean on is the widowed father of a little girl in her preschool class. His own wounds still healing, Trek Blue needs Annelise as much as she needs him.

Annelise discovers that Trek is another path to happiness…but can she turn her back on everything she's been taught?

The Light at Dawn

No matter how dark the night, hope is reborn at dawn.

It wasn't just her marriage that crumbled in the wake of unspeakable tragedy, it was her entire life. Even though five years had passed since she lost Evan, Angelia White was still picking up the pieces. Getting involved in a cause she could pour her broken heart into was just another part of the healing process.

The wounds were too fresh for Mark Lyon to keep his grip on reality. Everything he thought he knew and believed was obliterated when he lost Ashleigh, along with his heart. The only way he could pick up the pieces was to fight for a way to prevent any other parent from ever suffering such merciless pain.

Two heartbroken parents enduring the darkest of nights.
Two wounded souls waiting for the light at dawn.

A Million Little Stars (coming in 2020)

Women's Fiction

Fat Girl

**All Claire wants is a thin body and her dream man.
Is that too much to ask?**

With fresh ink on her divorce papers and a new job on the horizon, Claire Sterling is tired of being the Fat Girl. With the help of her gay best friend, a body image coach, a new fitness regime, and lots of wine and snark, she sets out to find her Happily Ever After just in time for her fortieth birthday.

Will she get the body and the man of her dreams, or is she forever destined to be the Fat Girl?

Green Castles

Inspired by true events, Green Castles tells the story of three former high school best friends; Jennifer, Kat, and Michelle; who are reunited in their small Indiana hometown when Jennifer's daughter loses her battle with mitochondrial disease. Through a series of flashbacks to their teen days in the late 1980's/early 1990's, the three women learn about resilience, forgiveness, and just how strong the bonds of family and friendship truly are.

Romantic Comedy

Romance in Rehoboth Series

Book 1: Music Man (coming in 2020—this Book #1 replaces *Fat Girl*, which was previously the first book in the series) – Claire & Jack's Story

Claire was nervous about getting involved in another serious relationship right after her divorce, but there's just something about Jack. Is it the beard? The flannel lumberjack look? Or the guitar? After all, every girl dreams of dating a rock star, even a girl who's just turned the Big 4-0.

Jack loved music since he was a kid, and he always dreamed of working in the music industry. When life got in the way of him making it big as a singer/songwriter, he settled for a career teaching music, including giving piano lessons to a certain redhead named Claire that he was falling head over heels for.

But his big break may have finally come...at exactly the wrong time.

Book 2: The Flip – Sonnet & Drew's Story

Aunt Penny's beach house isn't the only thing getting flipped in this hilarious romantic comedy!

Andrew and Sonnet hated each other in high school. Always rivals for the best grades and top academic honors, there was no love lost between these two nerds after graduation.

Ten years later, they're both named heirs to property in coastal Delaware after the passing of its owner, Penelope Vaughn, who was Andrew's great aunt and Sonnet's beloved next door neighbor growing up. The quaint beach cottage needs serious work before going on the market.

Andrew and Sonnet are both willing to bury the hatchet in exchange for drills and saws, especially since they stand to make a pretty penny with the beachfront property, which will finance Drew's dream of opening a business and Sonnet's plan to earn her doctorate in astrophysics. But when they face a multitude of home improvement obstacles, will these two former adversaries be able to pull off a successful flip?

Or did Great Aunt Penny have something else in mind all along?

Book 3: Plot Twist – Lindy & Meric's Story

If you think what's happening on stage is entertaining…you should see what's happening BACKSTAGE!

A brand new show is coming to Rehoboth Beach! Jack and Claire (yes, THAT Claire) Reilly have written an original musical, and they have the perfect cast. Plus, there's pirates. Who doesn't love pirates?

Meric Chandler is a neurotic, introverted accountant by day, but at night he transforms into a magnetic leading man whose voice makes all the girls swoon. Just getting over a divorce, he has sworn off backstage romances. After all, that's how he met his EX wife.

Lindy Larson prefers to stay behind the scenes, but her girlfriends convince her to audition for a new local theater production. She has a stunning voice but plans to blend in as much as possible, which isn't easy to do when you're the awkward plus-size girl with two left feet.

While backstage romances are to be expected, they don't usually shut down the entire production. But you know what they say: the show must go on!

Book 4: Badge Bunny – Brynne & Chris's Story

Looks can be deceiving in this hilarious enemies-to-lovers romcom complete with a shocking secret hobby, a heavy metal playlist, and an uninvited wedding guest!

Chris Everson has a pretty sweet life: a great job as a state trooper, lots of buddies to hang out with, and he lives at the beach. What could be better? But he's harboring a secret--a secret that doesn't fit with his whole tough guy cop persona. He's gone to great lengths to keep his secret from his guy friends AND the women he dates.

Brynne Miller's job as an ER doctor means she's always meeting cops. In fact, she's dated so many that her friends call her "Badge Bunny." But she will never date Chris Everson. Nope. Not a chance. He managed to piss her off within two seconds of meeting him...and first impressions are everything.

Aren't they?

Book 5: Wedding War – Hannah & Jason's Story

All's fair in love and war...and this is war.

Jason Friday's family business has kept the grooms of Delmarva in style for over forty years. Hannah Robinson's family has been doing the same for brides for nearly thirty.

A squabble over twenty years ago turned the two families into mortal enemies. As their businesses grew, their rivalry only became more cutthroat...until Über Brides sets up shop in Rehoboth Beach. This bridal superstore chain is known for slashing prices, squeezing every drop of discounts from their vendors, and running family-owned shops out of business.

The days of the Fridays and Robinsons serving the brides and grooms of Delmarva are numbered unless Jason and Hannah can band together to run Über Brides out of Rehoboth Beach. Can they manage to work together and ignore their growing attraction to each other? Or will they lose both their jobs and their families when they succumb to their desires?

Book 6: Stage Mom – Larissa & Mateo's Story

A mom who'll never give up fighting for her special needs daughter...
A "nice guy" who finally learns to take a stand...
Larissa and Mateo's worlds collide in Stage Mom!

Everything about Larissa Emerson is strong.
Her personality.
Her snark.
Her aversion to men after one too many disappointments.
Her unwavering fight to ensure her special needs daughter is treated like any other girl--a fight that ramps up when she begs to compete in a beauty pageant.

Mateo Flores is in his first year of heading up the Little Miss Rehoboth pageant, and he's not about to screw it up. He knew he'd be dealing with stereotypical pageant moms, but he never saw this one coming. She hits him like a hurricane, all strength and beauty and attitude.

How can he say no to a force of nature like Larissa Emerson?

Book 7: Shark Bite (coming in 2020)

Made in United States
Troutdale, OR
05/21/2024